S P I N E

❧

JOHN PATRICK HIGGINS

Sagging
Shorts

© 2025 by John Patrick Higgins

All Rights Reserved.

Set in Mrs Eaves XL with LaTeX.

ISBN: 978-1-963846-34-8 (paperback)
ISBN: 978-1-963846-35-5 (ebook)
Library of Congress Control Number: 2025931411

Sagging Meniscus Press
Montclair, New Jersey
saggingmeniscus.com

To Annie and Tom Higgins,
who won't get to read this.
I miss you both every day.

"I got no business going to a club.
I'm a terrible dancer.
I got a bad back."

—Ad-Rock

Skeleton Key

SPINE

Wince Cycle: Repeat

MY BACK PAGES

I WAS STILL drunk when I reached the physio's office. I'd been at a book launch the night before. Red wine was flowing, speeches were made. Somebody did a song. My friend Shirley was launching her book, and I thought it would be nice to support her. Also, I never go to book launches and I never network. Afterwards I remembered why. Five glasses in, I was introduced to Shirley's publisher. I immediately started talking about what kissing a ghost might be like.

Of course.

She looked sceptical from the outset. A chic Dubliner in her middle years, in a casual suit and vegan trainers, she was a woman who was always going to be sceptical of me, but even so, going in with the "frenching a phantom" gambit was an error of judgement. There *was* a reason: there'd been a reference to a ghostly kiss in the first draft of Shirley's book, but she'd removed it as the story changed, rendering the scene bizarre and irrelevant. But the novel I'm currently writing is chockful of spectral trysts—the title is *How Ghosts Affect Relationships*, after all. It became very clear to me, very quickly, this woman had no time at all for metaphysical mucking about.

"They don't exist," she said.

"I know," I said, "but imagine trying to kiss one. What would it feel like? What are they made of? Are their clothes made of the same stuff they are? Do the clothes come off?"

I was now undressing ghosts.

"But they don't exist," she said.

"I KNOW," I said, "but they are a *thing*. A thing in literature. A thing in culture. In human storytelling. C'mon."

"I'm not really interested in ghost stories. I publish Young Adult books."

I was flummoxed. I don't believe in ghosts—despite having seen two—but I'm *interested* in them. Who isn't interested in ghosts? This woman. Not having it, not one little bit. I dug a bit deeper, trying to get her to imagine the physical presence of a ghost. Would it be like the membranous skin of a poached egg? Or powdery, like an airbag deploying in your face? But the wine was kicking in, and I couldn't remember the word for airbag, so I had to mime it. I can still remember the look on her p. a.'s face, her mouth a perfect "o" of horror, eyes wide, as I continued my sauced-up charade.

Dear God.

I went outside. The party was breaking up, so I stood near some people who were vaping on the street. It was still early, so I swung by a bar and met some friends. On the way home I picked up a bottle of wine. The memory of my networking clung to me like an amorous phantom, coming on a bit too strong.

When I got into the physiotherapist's the next morning things were still a bit blurry, sweaty and stinky.

I'd had a bad back. Agony at the base of my spine, like a belt of magma, sparking fireworks into my thighs. Everything was difficult. Getting out of bed was laborious, involving rolling first onto my hip, then slowly jackknifing upward, before levering into the vertical, and feeling as if some tendril might snap at any moment, my legs falling uselessly to the floor, torso hovering in the air like a tailor's dummy. Climbing out of the bath was an impossibility, and saw me lying in the tub, hairy and trapped as a spider. Around the house, I became stiff and clumsy, dropping everything I picked up and abandoning it, because there was no way I could ever retrieve it again. Shattered mugs littered my kitchen floor, a slalom to be negotiated carefully and slowly, because everything was done carefully and slowly now. Even brushing my teeth involved worrying lateral movement I could feel lurching in the lava of my tortured spine.

I didn't know what was causing the bad back. Susan wondered if it might be my new office chair (offering my lower back support for the first time) or our mattress (which we've had for a couple of years without any problems). Could it have been my new walking boots? Or that I'd been walking five miles a day since I got them. Or possibly, that I favour my right hand entirely when writing (the pain belts the base of my spine but seems to be focused on the left side).

I doubted very much it was any of those things. It was more likely that, when the day was done, and it was time for me to relax after a gruelling day's typing, I lay down on my left side on the couch, typing into the laptop on the small table in front of me, as I watched horror films on television. And I did this for hours, lying in what's come to be known as *The Roman Position*, as though I were Nero at the trough, chowing down on grapes and fermented fish guts.

I may have to sit up straight in future to avoid searing pain, if it's not already too late. But I love slouching. I adore backsliding. You'll always find me down the back of the sofa at parties, with my friends the loose change, the crumbs, the winning lottery ticket.

No more. I needed to straighten up and fly right. I intended to go out for my hike. It'd probably rain. Good. I deserved it, with my narrow shoulders and slovenly spine. It was time to iron out those kinks with exercise and general misery. Comfort be damned.

In fact, I didn't go. I got about five hundred yards before the bubbling pyroclastic flow at the base of my spine became too much, and I crawled home. I didn't need exercise after all. I needed a medical intervention. I needed a lab-coated professional to wade into my inky depths. I'm pretty sure I needed drugs. Lovely drugs.

I filled in a self-referral form for an NHS physiotherapist. The National Health Service remains the greatest thing the United Kingdom ever did, a genuinely brilliant idea. Everything else has been compromised by murky politics and self-interest, all that Old Empire business, where we nicked other countries' stuff and killed everybody. But the NHS was fantastic: free healthcare for everyone in the country. You no longer had to die just because you were poor. A factory worker and the Duke of Argyll would, in theory, get the same medical care. The effect was extraordinary. After the horrors of the first part of the 20th Century, where World Wars had killed millions, this was the establishment of anti-war: this time everyone would live.

It's so great, such genuinely good news, such an inarguable boon to the country, that many, many politicians would like to get rid of it. They don't say that, of course. We *love* our NHS in the UK, and nothing bad can happen to it. But there's no profit in it, and over the last few years, cool and unsympathetic, the Tories regarded the American healthcare system with envious eyes, and slowly and surely drew their plans against us.

They underfunded, underpaid, allowed hospital buildings to collapse through neglect and lack of resources, and then condemned doctors and nurses for protesting—very selfish when people are dying—or when they left the profession because the pressure of the job was unbearable. Then they could say that, sadly, the NHS wasn't working, and we needed to look at a different system, a system that unsurprisingly would make their friends and donors exceedingly rich.

Rich from the bodies of the sick, like medical leeches. Though medical leeches are useful.

I wasn't expecting much when I filled in the on-line "self-referral" form—it's impossible to see a doctor now—and pinged it off into the ether. People on social media were gloomier still. "I filled one out in March and didn't see a physio till Christmas," said one, micturating freely over my French fries.

The processing time would be five weeks, at least, and there was no knowing when a viable date would become available after that period. Either way I was going to have to sustain a bad back for well over a month, and while it was agony now, I wasn't sure I could keep it up all that time. Maybe I could exercise without warming up or lift with my back not my knees to top up the agony. Though I'm of an age now where turning over in bed too quickly can seriously compromise my vertebrae. I wouldn't have to worry. I'd had an abundance of sudden and crippling bad backs over the last few years. I could afford to waste one. Another would just take its place, like Pez in the dispenser.

I didn't have to worry anyway. I received a letter in just over a week, advising me to call them. I did so, gave them my "Paris number" (I have no idea what a Paris number is, but it was printed on the letter, so I read out my Paris number) and told them what colour my letter was (yellow) and they gave me an appointment for the following week, at a medical centre half a mile from my house.

Social media was appalled. How the hell had I pulled off this coup?

Suck it up, guys.

In the intervening three weeks, from pressing send on the completed form, to turning up drunk to the appointment, the bad back had largely sorted itself out. Luckily, I had a lot of historical issues to talk about with the physio. My legs are different lengths for a start. I wouldn't be wasting anyone's time.

BABY'S GOT BACK ACHE

PLENTY OF FAMOUS people have bad backs. It's quite chic to have a slipped disc or lumber with your lumbar. We're all doing it. Cellulite is so last year, darling. Here are a few famous people who spent a *lot* of money on a mattress.

1. Sarah Michelle Gellar

Buffy the Vampire Slayer has scoliosis. She treats it with treadmill running, Pilates and face-kicking the undead while listening to the *worst* bands in the world down at *The Bronze*. The worst bands. My band could get a gig in *The Bronze*. My band.

Cibo Matto were on one week. They were okay. But *Sprung Monkey*? *Velvet Chain*? *Lotion* gets a pass for having the ultimate '90s band name. Every town in the world harboured a band named *Lotion* in the '90s.

Backman and Rubbin'

2. Jerry Lewis

Jerry suffered a back injury doing a pratfall from a piano at the Sands hotel in Las Vegas in 1965. He manages his pain with "a spinal cord stimulator". According to the *Deuk Spine Institute*, this apparatus does not work. Furthermore, it can cause spinal fluid leaks and spinal headaches. Yikes! Then again, the Deuk Spine Institute is based in Melbourne, Florida, so now I don't know what to believe. Also, Jerry's convinced it works and it's his spine.

There's nothing funny about Jerry's back injury. So at least he's consistent.

3. Usain Bolt

I have no idea if Usain Bolt is still the fastest man in the world. But at one point he was, which rather raises the bar for bad back malingerers like me, because Usain has a bad back. Specifically, he also has scoliosis, his spine curving to the right, and his right leg half an inch shorter than his left. Something of an over-achiever in the bad back community, then. I feel for those other athletes, torturing themselves with diets as complex and detailed as a Medieval astrology chart, when Usain just rocks up to the starting blocks with a bucket full of chicken and a lopsided stride. He's finished running before the greasy fingerprints on his race bib have even stained. C'mon Usain, they cry, bent double and retching at the finish line, you're making us look like dicks. But Usain can't hear them—he's already miles away doing a lucrative advertising campaign for Unilever.

4. Batman

In the comic book series, *Knightfall*, Batman has his back broken by the super-villain Bane whom, I think it's safe to say, lifts. I steer clear of the manosphere, but both Batman and Bane are clearly *Sigma Males*. They go their own way. But when Sigma Males meet, well, spines and noses get put out of joint. This is from the comics—I haven't seen the films—I know Tom Hardy's Bane is in one of them, but I don't know if he breaks Ben Affleck's back.

While researching this bit, I came across a Batman villain called *Film Freak*. Film Freak's gimmick is that he commits crimes based on scenes from famous films. That's it. He has no powers. He's effectively an evil set designer. Imagine the planning he puts into getting Batman to a crossroads in a cornfield so he can strafe him with bullets from a crop-dusting plane (*North by Northwest*), or onto a building site at the bottom of a hill, severing the Dark Knight's head with a sheet of glass (*The Omen*), or pretending to be the host of *This is Your Dish*, so he can serve up Batmite and Ace The Bat-Hound in a couple of pies (*Theatre of Blood*).

Anyone who's ever had to plan a surprise birthday party for a relative, knows exactly what an organisational nightmare it is to get anyone to a specific place at a specific time, and in secret, and that's just positioning a tipsy uncle in the back room of a pub, not manipulating the world's greatest detective into an exact copy of the cantina from *Star Wars*. So many supporting artists too. Even if he's only paying Equity minimum, it's a lot of cash. And there's the musicians—these people have a union, Film Freak. They're not paying to play. So, it's a lot of time, a lot of money, and Batman may never even show. I admire your commitment, Film Freak, but is this really the best use of your skills?

I'd like to see the comic where Film Freak waits patiently in a booby-trapped life-size diorama of *The Breakfast Club* library, and Batman never turns up. Five in the morning, Film Freak calls it a day. He stretches, lights a cigarette, looks at the wasted perfection of his creation. It really is *exactly* like the library in *The Breakfast Club*. Correct in every detail. He picks up a perfect replica of one of Judd Nelson's discarded cigarette butts and realises it's more about the dioramas than the murder of the Caped

Crusader these days. This is his true calling. Maybe he could get into installations or something . . .

I hope you make it, Film Freak. You do good work.

Anyway, in the comics, Batman gets better from his snapped spine. One of his friends has mystical powers and they're able to just . . . fix his broken back. Which is nice. Problem solved.

5. Batgirl

Batgirl wasn't so lucky. The Joker shot Barbara Gordon through the spine, resulting in her paraplegia. He must have been having an off day because that's just not funny, you fucking Edge Lord. Barbara then becomes wheelchair-bound super-genius Oracle—you can't keep a good superhero down. But you would think, wouldn't you, that her good friend and mystically enhanced smashed-back survivor, Batman, might say, "Oh, actually, Babs, I know a guy . . ."

But he doesn't. Batman is SUCH a dick.

6. St. Gemma Galgani

The patron saint of bad backs is Gemma Galgani. She also covers pharmacists, students and paratroopers, which is a wide brief. Her Father was a pharmacist, which could have been a bit awkward. You don't want to have to pray to your own daughter for God's intercession. Luckily, Gemma was orphaned at nineteen, long before she was canonised, so that bit of social ickiness was avoided. Phew.

Galgani chatted to her guardian angel, to Jesus and Mary, and to the angel Gabriel. She also had stigmata and reportedly levitated. Apparently, her younger sister would mock her during these ecstatic periods, which is a strangely human note in the life story of a saint. The eye-rolling younger sibling at the breakfast table, like Jan Brady. "Gemma, Gemma, Gemma—it's always about her!"

Gemma died of T.B. on Holy Saturday, 1903. She was twenty-five. I can find no reason at all, anywhere in her life, as to why she's the patron saint of bad backs. St Lucy is the patron saint of the blind because, before her martyrdom, she had her eyes gouged out. I can follow that train of thought. (In paintings she's always depicted with a dish with a pair of loose eyes in it—BUT SHE STILL HAS HER OWN EYES! Whose eyes are they, Lucy? Whose eyes? They're on a tray. She looks like a cinema usherette with the creepiest snack selection you've ever seen.) But Saint Gemma Galgani seems to have no association with bad backs at all. Or paratroopers, for that matter.

THERAPY?

I GOT LOST on the way to the Therapy Centre. This was particularly poor as I'd gone out two days earlier to locate it. On that day I'd walked there in half an hour.

Today though, once again woozy with booze, head swimming, breath like Kola Kubes, I took the bus and, on alighting, walked past the Therapy Centre and halfway into town, before realising my mistake and doubling back. I arrived drunk, sweaty, out of breath and late.

Sitting in the plastic school chair in reception, my tracksuit bottoms stuck to it. When I'm called by the physio there is an audible slurp as I vacate the seat. I've left behind a wet patch the size and shape of a horseshoe crab for the next unsuspecting slipped-discer.

Sorry.

The physio is nice. A bearded youth with the look of someone whose interest in the workings of the human body was fostered in the world of Gaelic Association Football. He politely ignored the alcoholic fumes wafting off me like smoke from a cartoon bomb and started on the lengthy questionnaire I'd filled in about my medical history. I love filling these in because I get to tick the "no" box to every ailment. Is it a blameless life or just that I haven't been to the doctor for years, and have no idea what's lurking within? Regardless, as far as I know, I'm fine.

My therapist is dead impressed when I loftily described myself as a "writer"—an excuse for my round shoulders and poor posture—and gives an audible "fuck" when I show him my knee scar. It is quite impressive. From the Evel Knievel school.

He then hurts me in various precise and practiced ways.

"Does that hurt?"

"I think you know it does, Cian."

I can do all his exercises with relative ease. He has me touching my toes and is complimentary about my strength, as though I were the stubborn skin on a rice pudding he thought his spoon would puncture with ease.

I'm still drunk. The session is a blur. I crack jokes. I groan and sweat as I go through the exercises. I remember I'm wearing a Compeed pad on my heel because of a cloche-sized blister and become embarrassed about it. It's an inglorious start.

He sends me off with a leaflet of black-and-white photos of exercises to do. They remind me of a book I owned in the late '70s that was supposed to teach me Tae Kwon-Doe. I never learned Tae Kwon-Doe. A seven-year-old boy in his pyjamas doing high kicks strikes terror in the heart of precisely no one, unless they still have PTSD from watching *Billy Elliot*. But these exercises are doable. I WILL be supple again. Lissom, even. Able to get out of the bath unassisted. My shoelaces are practically within reach.

I have three sessions with Cian, and I'm hung over for all of them. I swear I'm not doing this on purpose. The sessions are at different times over the weeks—there's no set pattern—and they all seem to be on the morning after I've an appointment to drink. Cian must think I'm a night owl who smells permanently of Pear Drops. Or maybe he's met drunks before.

Oh, and it's Cain, not Cian, as I previously thought. Cain. Isn't that like being called Pontius or Barrabas? It's not one of the traditional names you'd lift from the Bible to give a baby, though I'd argue Herod is worse.

Still, I try out the "You're Cain, and I'm unable," gambit, and it dies on its arse. Cain just looks confused. I mean, why would you name your child after history's first fratricidal nutter and not tell him the story? I suppose he might start asking questions. He might start looking with envious eyes at his brother. Why is the smell of his cookery so pleasing to the Almighty? Probably best not to open that can of Biblical worms.

I've had three sessions with Cain, and they're all the same: ten minutes of knee flexing, jokes about the brittle ineptitude of my body, as it crackles and pops with each slight adjustment, and then I'm out the door with a photocopy of the exercises I'm obliged to do.

But on one of these occasions, Cain asks me if I'd consider doing a Pilates course, which he thinks would be great for my core, and apparently having a half decent core is a desirable thing. So, I sign up. It's months away, anyway.

SPORTING ATTIRE (WHILE SPORTING A TYRE)

───────◆───────

I QUEUE in the same dingy healthcare centre I had the physiotherapy. I'd had a phone call confirming I'd be joining a referral class, and showed up in an anorak, track-suit bottoms, and powder blue Adidas Gazelles. This is not my standard look. Over the past year or so I feel I've capitulated in matters sartorial. I live in Northern Ireland where it rains. It always rained here, of course, but climate change has now made the water wetter. It's also windy, so I've faced years of degloved umbrellas, their spokes exposed, dripping in my hallway like eviscerated bats. In Northern Ireland everything has cultural weight, and umbrellas are associated with Orange Men, marching about like they own the place which, increasingly, they don't. Umbrellas are also associated with the English, those watery imperial bastards, with their soup-strainer moustaches and deep pockets full of your cultural artefacts. And, of course, I am English, a fact I don't want or need to advertise.

So, finally, after a decade or so of trying not to develop gills in the face of this extraordinary, saturating assault, I bought a coat with a hood. It's black. Just black. Nothing written on it, no logo. It looks okay. Too many zips, and too many tassels on the zips. But it's discreet, functional, unobtrusive and keeps the rain off my crowning glory.

But it doesn't breathe. It features no natural fibres or Gore-Tex technology. I feel I'm just wrapped in cling-film like an exhibitionist mummy. After ten minutes, my arms are soaking wet, even when my hair is dry. I haven't bought another, better coat, as I think it might be a good way to lose weight in the long run. It's certainly an excellent way to ruin your shirt.

The trainers are also new. I bought Adidas because they're the only trainers I like as they're the only ones that look good. I think I fell out of love with The Cure when Robert Smith started galumphing about in his big, puffy high tops. I suppose it fitted his late-eighties night-mare teddy-bear aesthetic, but it wasn't for me. I knew I'd never be able to meet girls wearing footwear that looked like I was retaining a lot of fluid below the ankle-line.

Adidas Gazelles are sharp, colourful, suede and, crucially, I don't associate them with sport. And I figured, as I got older and was obliged to start doing things I didn't want to do, like exercising and cutting down on the endless excess, and during my lengthy periods of hospitalisation, sports shoes might be useful. They look better with pyjamas than brogues do, and there's less click-clacking around on sticky hospital lino.

I went shoe shopping with my friend, Joe. I sprung it on him, because I knew he'd be uncomfortable with the homoerotic frisson of two men shopping for footwear together, but I needed a second opinion. I'm virginal in the world of sportswear. I'd picked out some eye-popping powder blue Gazelles from the meagre selection in J.D. Sports. They were almost iridescent: lapis lazuli crushed in a mortar, dazzling next to their lumpen companions. They were the only shoes in the shop as far as I was concerned. But this was problematic. I do not dazzle. I am grey and middle-aged. I'm drifting toward portliness. I have great hair, sure, but everything south of my wrinkly pink forehead is on the slide. Could I get away with these beautiful shoes? Or would I look like a vagrant trampling peonies in the park?

So, I drafted in a clearly uncomfortable Joe to give me his opinion, with the proviso we could go for a manly pint afterwards, which seemed to mollify him.

I tried them on. There was a general feeling in the room that they were magnificent, I looked like the Sun King wearing them, so I bought them, and we went to the pub, and I remembered to take them home with me at the end of the night, which I was both surprised and pleased by.

On my way home from the pub—and the seal broken, so to speak—I popped into the off-license for some more beer.

Yes, there does seem to be a lot of beer being drunk in this story. Perhaps it's subtext, who can say?

I've been going to this off-license for many years and knew the senior staff to make pleasantries with. I'm never comfortable with the transactional relationship: customer vs vendor. I either feel like King Charles on a walkabout, asking little people what they do, or I'm fiercely intimidated, like Julia Roberts in the posh shop in *Pretty Woman*. These are my two positions, and I don't enjoy either of them. It's called being English, I suppose.

But an off-license is my place of power. I know what I'm doing in an off-license. I know more about the beers and the wine, the spirits and the salted snack treats, than the staff do. I can relax here. I can talk about the weather, or crack jokes and say hello and goodbye. All the things. But today, as I queued with my bottles of Kingfisher, my big, square J.D. Sports bag was over my shoulder, unmistakably containing a new pair of trainers. There was a boy serving the woman in front of me, being trained by another boy. And the senior boy clocked my bag and snorted with derision. His eyes met mine and his face froze into a rictus. But I saw him, and he saw I saw him, and we both knew what had taken place. He had sneered at the idea of me doing a sport, any sport. He was right to, but he didn't know that.

I resolved never to return. I'd been buying booze from this gaff for the best part of a decade, thousands of my pounds had flooded their tills, and now this fucking oaf, who wouldn't have sprung his first pube when I first started patronising the shop, was laughing at the notion of an elderly booze hound slipping on a pair of high-end sneakers and attempting to prolong his life. Fuck you. By making me veto my local wine-and-beer emporium, you've made it inconvenient for me to buy alcohol. The trainers had already started making me fitter. Good job, Adidas.

Besides, this fucker was half my age and twice as wide as me. He'd be found—dead at 38—in a parked car with a half-eaten kebab in his lap, chilli sauce all over his cold, blue lips. Or so I like to think.

I still walk past the off-licence on my daily walks around the neighbourhood and see him boxed in behind the counter in his empty shop. The first couple of times he waved when he saw me pass. Not anymore.

The poor fool. He hasn't a clue he's in a bitter feud with a man he barely knows about a pair of shoes he's never seen. I pity him.

I'm at my first Pilates class, I'm the star of the show. I'm teacher's pet. If I'd shown up with an apple, it couldn't have gone better. There are several reasons for this. I've got great trainers. I'm wearing a cool t-shirt (it features the album cover for Can's *Future Days*—I don't expect people to know the record, but it's a cool image). My hair is looking splendid. But mainly, it's because I'm the youngest person here, I can bend, and I've done Pilates before. My instructor is the most Irish person I've ever met. She's like an Irish woman from an American Western. I can see John Wayne carrying her out a saloon over his shoulder, as she kicks and kicks and says, "If tis a foight ye'll be wanting, you've just met the foighting O'Hooley clan!"

Her name is Caoilfhionn, which is pronounced "Keelin", and means "slender and fair" in Irish. She is slender. We'll see how fair she is as she dishes out the punishments over the forthcoming weeks. There's a Saint Caoilfhionn—feast day February third—and according to the *Martyrdom of Donegal*, she was canonised for winning "the esteem of her sister nuns, by her exactness to every duty, as also, by her sweet temper, gentle, confiding disposition and unaffected piety".

Wait, sorry, what?

She was made a saint for being nice. Is that it? I imagine saints Lawrence (grilled to death), Cassian (stabbed to death by children), and Bartholomew (skinned alive) might have been a bit miffed at her smooth journey towards beatification. Even local celebrity Saint Dymphna had to be beheaded by her own father before the halos were handed out. Saint Caoilfhionn must have had a *spectacularly* confiding disposition.

This Caoilfhionn, the Pilates instructor, is an upbeat, chatty redhead, speckled in freckles. She hands out stickers, our names written on them in a charmingly naïve hand, which we stick on. There are ten of us, in varying states of decrepitude, including three men, which she seems excited by.

"I don't get many men," she says. The other two—probably in their sixties—are called Eddie and Freddie. Neither has sports gear on. They do the exercises in the same grey socks I used to wear to school. I go barefoot. You get better purchase.

It's a small room. There are too many of us. As I go about my poses I hit, variously, a bin, a treadmill and the face of the woman next to me.

I'm trying to relax and find my neutral space, but the NHS yoga mat smells of unknown arses, and the stereo is playing a dance version of *Here Comes the Sun*, which is not much enhanced by synthesised pan pipes.

As Caoilfhionn goes through her well-practiced routine, I find my experience of other Pilates classes paying off. I can do anything she asks, easily and quickly. I'm also right at the front of the class, like the big lick I am. When she asks if anyone has ever done Pilates before, my hand shoots up. What a swot.

We go through the various first-timer positions—no *Warrior Pose* here, not even a *Downward Dog*—we're doing the *Shoulder Bridge* and the *Clam*. This is how you do the former:

— Inhale to prepare.
— Exhale, and gently roll your lower back into the mat, scooping your tailbone upwards and continuing to peel your spine off the mat, bone by bone, until you're resting on your shoulder blades.
— Inhale, holding the shoulder bridge position.
— Exhale and lower the shoulder bridge by lowering one bone at a time to the mat, beginning with

the uppermost vertebrae and finishing to return
to neutral position.

— Do this ten times.

I do this ten times with practiced ease. My physiotherapist proscribed exactly this exercise when I went
to see him. I've been doing it for weeks! I'm not even
breaking a sweat, while all about me the old and infirm
are puffing and wheezing, their calcified limbs groaning,
then crashing into the mats in clouds of dust and invec-
tive. If I could have been chewing on a blade of grass or
taking a casual bite from a crunchy Pink Lady, I'd have
done so. By the time we move onto *hundreds*—basically
very fast jazz hands—I'm thinking, during the *rest position*,
I may become a Yogi. This is a piece of piss. I'm a natural,
at least in this room. I was zinging.

Then I went out into the pissing rain at rush hour on
East Belfast's Newtownards Road. It's cold and dark, as
traffic jams and ambulances scream past. It was like I'd
been on a lovely holiday, toes stretching into white sand
under azure skies, only for a begloved customs official to
use me like a Ventriloquist Dummy in a lightless, airless
airport backroom.

Namaste, my arse.

YOGA PARTY

SOMETHING'S HAPPENED. I'm not sure what it is. I get in the room for the second Pilates appointment—I'm wearing my *I Would Prefer Not To* t-shirt, which often excites great interest in supermarket cashiers, who may not get the reference to "Bartleby the Scrivener" but can very much appreciate the sentiment—and I'm shit at Pilates.

Now, I *am* shit at Pilates, okay. I know that. In this room I'm very much grading on a curve, and last week I was, at best, least worst. This week I'm not even that. These traitorous bastards must have been diligently doing their exercises. They're sliding effortlessly into rest position, their feet and knees hip distance apart, their ribcages softening into the mat, shoulder blades brought down to the neck and shoulders. And I look like a sofa someone's dropped from a third-storey window into a car park. I'm unmalleable and stiff, great news if I was an erection, but not so good if I'm slowly drawing up through the pelvic floor to engage my deep abdominal muscles. My increasingly deep abdominal muscles. I mean, they're in there somewhere, but finding them is like trying to uncover the Oak Island Mystery.

Caoilfhionn has noticed. At one point, to sort out my posture, she wordlessly sticks a foam rubber ball between my knees, so they remain the appropriate distance from one another. My attempt at the clam meets a similarly silent intervention, as she grabs my hips and rolls them over, so the exercise I'm doing instantly becomes much harder. I've been shirking, on top of everything else.

By the time I get into the rhythm of it, it's over and we're all putting our shoes back on. Damn it all to hell.

I determine to walk home, to punish my already sore knee and hip. The sky overhead is bruising, a lovely bit of pathetic fallacy—thanks sky gods—as I beat myself up over my frozen hips, my rusted joints, my flabby and useless core. I feel terrible about myself. I need something to happen, and to happen immediately.

Oh, wait . . .

DOG MAN STAR

SOMETIMES HEROES wear tracksuit bottoms and an
anorak.

I'm on my way back from my Pilates class when I
bump into my friend, Lesley. There are certain people
you can meet without seeing them for a long time and
there's no lag, no awkwardness, you just slip cleanly back
into the rhythm. Lesley's one of them. I haven't seen her
in well over a year, but we chat as if it had been yesterday.
Today we're mainly slagging off the fashions of young
people. And fair play to young people, with your mullets,
moustaches, your sleeves of tattoos, gym-sculpted bodies and Simon-Bates-metal-rim specs, you've found that
sartorial sweet spot, elegantly calibrated to offend me. It
almost makes me proud. We post-punk jumble-dippers,
with our ratted-up hair and dead men's coats, our flicks
of kohl and perforated Levis, we thought we were *it*. We'd
seen punk. What else can you show us? How can you offend us? Oh. Okay, yeah. That's awful. Very good. You got
me.

Weird Al Yankowich as the fashion touchstone for a generation. Brilliant.

As Ian Faith from *Spinal Tap* would say, "You look like an Australian's nightmare."

Lesley and I were chewing the fat over these fashion foibles, when I saw a shadow flit past her shoulder. A large black dog trotted over the Newtownards Road and wandered into someone's driveway. Now, normally when I see a black dog, I have a bit of a cry and a lie down with a cool pillow over my eyes, but I was pretty sure this one was real.

"Did you see that?" I said.

"See what?" said Lesley.

"A big black dog just ran across the road. I can't see an owner anywhere."

"No," she said, accurately, as she had her back to the scenario.

"Oh, there it is."

The dog emerged from the driveway and started padding along the pavement towards us. Lesley turned in time to see it stop sniffing the curb and step directly into traffic. The Newtownards is a busy arterial road, this was rush-hour and dark and the dog was black. Lesley screamed, as a guy on a scooter swerved and stopped, and the bus behind him slammed on the brakes with a hydraulic whine. The dog, by some miracle, made it to the other side of the road, and was into someone else's driveway. The bus driver drove on, swearing from his cab window. The scooter bloke, clearly rattled, asked, "Is that your dog?" No, we replied.

"Christ, the only thing I saw was the reflective strip on its collar. Is it okay?" We thought it probably was okay, and he drove off again, quite slowly, just in case.

On the far side of the road the dog emerged from the garden it had been investigating and was back on the pavement. We couldn't believe its lack of common sense. The idiot had no concept of being run over and would clearly leap into the road again, should it suddenly have urgent business on the opposite side of the street, and it did seem to have something of a "grass is always greener" mindset. It was incredible it wasn't dead. It had already crossed the road twice in heavy traffic, but I feared three times would not be the charm. I knew it had a collar—it wasn't a stray—so it would probably be friendly if I could only get to the other side of the road before it threw itself under a bus.

The traffic was relentless. The nearest crossing point was five minutes away, but suddenly there was a gap in the traffic, and I hurled myself into it, running like a man who'd been working on his core for an hour. I made it to the other side of the road, past the beeping traffic, and grabbed the fool dog by the collar and into a hedge, as far from the curb as possible, Lesley close behind me.

There was a name on the collar. "Penny". Bad Penny. There was a phone number too, but Lesley didn't have her glasses, I had the wrong contact lenses in, and it was dark, so neither of us could read it. Scuppered by middle-age again. A young couple appeared and got involved. Their youthful eyes worked, and soon Lesley was phoning the owner who was both at home and nearby. (I worked out from her address that Penny crossed the road, in the dark, at rush hour, at least *three* times. Lucky Penny).

The owner arrived, jittery and thankful, explaining the dog escaped either because builders removed a fence, or her children let her out, and she took Penny, whose collar I was still holding and who had been squirming to get back and play with the traffic—a dog with a death wish—away. I said goodbye to the young people and Lesley, and we all went to our homes.

I thought about how nice everyone had been: the young people, who had been relatively well-dressed, the scooter guy, Lesley, even me, for a change. Normally, I don't like people but, in this instance, everyone had been delightful, helpful, kind, even brave. Is this dogs? Is this what dogs do? Even suicidal ones? Is this the dog effect?

On the way back home, I thought perhaps I should have been stern with that dog owner. She was very vague about why her dog was loose and hadn't even noticed she was gone. If Lesley and I hadn't been there, we could have been looking at real carnage, a low-budget version of the end of *An American Werewolf in London*.

But I was glad I hadn't been stern with her. She was so pleased to have poor, depressed Penny back, and everyone else had been so cool. So, just this once, I decided I wouldn't be a dick.

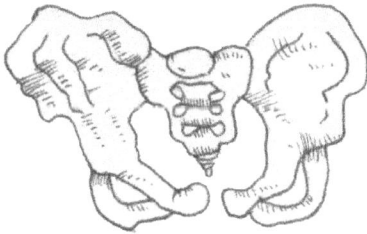

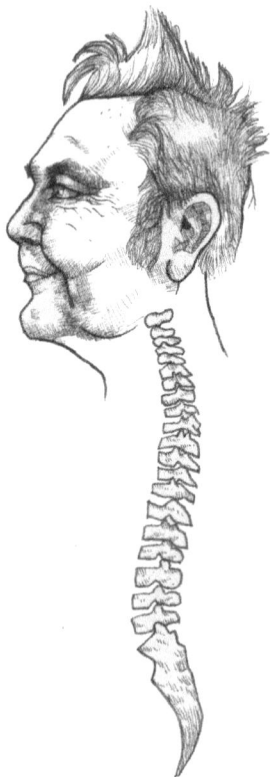

The Tingler

LET'S GET METAPHYSICAL

LET ME tell you a story . . .

I was on the beach, getting pummelled by the breakers at the water's edge. It was the first time I'd been in the sea for forty years and it felt amazing. Primal. Huge. Attacked by a ravening beast. I made it in up to my waist, and it repeatedly knocked me on my arse. There was soft, sucking shingle which quickly gave way to slippery, submerged rock, so I never went further than the silt line. But still, it felt fantastic, and I laughed manically as the tide repeatedly shrugged me off. You're powerless in the face of the sea. There's a reason why planet Earth is blue—we're Poseidon's bitch. And there's a reason the sailors of the past never learned to swim—there was no point. The sea will just swallow you. It is bigger and more terrifying than anything in nature. Retrieving a rubber brick from the bottom of the pool while wearing your pyjamas won't save you from rampaging Tiamat. I'd only breached the sea's white, lacy fringes and it had repeatedly beaten me down. It was thrilling but safe. Jeopardy, with stabilizers.

I sloped back up the beach, grinning, while a boy and a girl strolled down it. They were accompanied by two large, black dogs and one large, white towel. The couple were, perhaps, in their early twenties. She was blonde, he had dark hair and, if you were attempting to advertise a beach, or a new kitchen, or a Toyota Yaris or just about anything really, this would be the couple you'd choose. When she stripped to her bikini you could add Bodyform and '90s hip-hop to that list. They were a good-looking pair.

There was a large rock poking out of the sea, making a better job of defying the waves than I had. It looked like granite from the way it was broken up into sharp shelves and was shark's fin grey. The girl walked into the sea and towards the rock and pulled herself onto it. She found a handhold, then a foothold, and she was up, climbing its ridges as easily as a spiral staircase, then she was at the top, strolling about the jagged summit in bare feet, thirty feet above the water.

The wind was up, the breakers crashing. She's mad, I thought. To injury-averse people like me, who have lost teeth to cheese soufflés, clambering up a giant granite rock, nearly naked, and wandering about like it was your hotel balcony, is reckless beyond belief. I was in awe of her.

Without warning, and quite casually, she back-flipped off the rock and plunged into a shallow pool. She disappeared. There was barely a splash. Fucking hell. The pool was circled by jagged rocks and the seabed too was solid rock beyond the skirt of shingle. Fucking hell.

She reappeared, after an improbable length of time, seal-sleek and not bleeding from the head, striding up the beach like Botticelli's Venus, minus the big clam. She looked primordial, mythical. She'd done the bravest thing I'd ever seen anyone do, and for no reason. She did it because she could, and because she'd look amazing do-ing it. It was like something from a film, but a film in which I wouldn't be the protagonist, or the comic relief or even credited at all, unless it was something like "Fat Wet Beach Man with His Mouth Open". The story was else-where. The story was all her. As she swam in the sea with her two black dogs, I could see she'd be the star of her own great adventure. And as her boyfriend sat on a towel on the beach, I could tell he'd be written out after the first season.

Later, we returned to the beach and the tide had gone out. We could see the rock, taller now, and the pool she'd jumped into was ringed by a spiky, stone crown. The jump was even more dangerous than it had appeared. Susan pointed out the girl was probably local and might have been jumping from that rock for years, perhaps since she was a child. And I thought back to my own child-hood, and my dad trying to teach me to swim in the mu-nicipal baths, and how I'd clung onto him like a spider monkey, screaming, refusing to put my head under the water and how, eventually, he'd given up, and I'd never learned to swim properly, though I loved swimming now. I knew I didn't have it in me to leap from that rock. Even before all the damage, before the shattered limbs. I just wasn't brave. It wasn't in me.

And I'd never look that good in a bikini.

I'm a coward. What my late friend Doug would, and did, call a "shit-leg". I don't like fighting and haven't been in a fight since I was in primary school, and that was so long ago I don't even think they still call it primary school. Don't get me wrong—I've been beaten up plenty of times. But a fight implies two active participants, and after the first punch, I was rarely that involved, beyond being a human buffer in a freestyle display of Irish danc-ing. To this day, if I see a gang of three tough-looking schoolgirls hanging around a bus stop, I will cross the road, just to avoid the humiliating catcalls. Teenage girls are terrifying.

I wish I could say it's just physical cowardice too. One of the reasons for my late arrival on the scene of . . . well, *anything*, is my life-long inability to grasp the nettle. I never believed anything I did would be worth anybody's time. I've created things since I was a child and was too scared to share them with anyone until my forties. There were demo tapes I recorded and sent to nobody. Whole albums obscured beneath a sound-proof bushel. Novels written and carefully placed in drawers which were then locked, cemented over and dropped off a quay under cover of darkness. My plays unsent as draft emails. Film scripts lying idle round the house like teenagers on summer holiday. Years and years of hidden, shameful toil. The last person who worked this long and this hard on a project he told nobody about was Josef Fritzl.

I may take that joke out. It's in very poor taste. But you get the idea.

At forty I found myself widowed, jobless, and living alone in a new country. I thought, I'll give writing a go. I had nothing left to lose because I had nothing. I met a tsunami of long-deferred rejections, but no longer cared. Life, a lucky life I no longer felt I could squander, had galvanised me. There are worse things than someone telling you suck at writing. Especially if there are typos in the rejection letter.

It's shocking. I find it shocking now. It took Kelly's death, the death of my wife, whom I adored and who was the most powerfully alive person I'd ever met—she hummed with life—to be bitten out of the world by that awful fucking disease. You know the one, because when they die at thirty-six it's always *that* disease. It took that personal apocalypse, to make me finally get off my arse and do something. I find myself despicable. I want to kick sand in my own face, to administer an atomic wedgie. Nurples so purple you could make Caesar's toga out of them. I'm a creature curling in on itself, a blind invertebrate hiding in the cool sand, cowering from the sun. I did ultimately do something and continue to do things. But it took astonishing leverage. Matters were taken out of my hands.

The mystery remains: how does someone this spineless contrive to have a bad back? I have to starch my suits till they act as scaffolding.

It's a metaphor, John. There is no "yellow streak a mile wide" down your back. What would that even look like? You haven't got "jelly legs". Well, not both. It's possible to be afraid of failure, of mocking laughter and pointing fingers, and still have a touch of back trouble.

I'm living proof.

PHYSICAL JERKS

I'M IN THE RECEPTION AREA at the health centre where my Pilates class takes place. It's full of school-assembly chairs, single-moulded pieces of furniture that would survive a dropped atom bomb, the furniture of choice for a mutated cockroach society. The crowd is thin today. Not physically, there aren't many people here, but the ones that are fill the room like a gas, albeit a gas wearing un-branded sportswear. There are a couple of girls dressed in black and giggling with one another in what sounds like a private language but might just as easily be a Bal-lynahinch accent. It's only when they are called into see the podiatrist—the waiting room shares a podiatry, phys-iotherapy and Pilates clientele—I realise they're mother and daughter. I can see them, in a couple of years' time, touring the bars together: "People say we could be sis-ters," they'd say and, for once, people would be right.

The rest of the scant crowd melts away: ancient, blue-nosed men, staggering like zombies, and neat, stoic middle-aged women, whose faces have settled into tight-

L'homme du Sport

lipped masks over the years, as they've just got used to the pain. One of them I think I recognise from Pilates, but it's hard to know. In the class, you aren't really looking at anyone else but the instructor, and there are so many things to remember. Burying your shoulders into the mat, chin down, finding your neutral space, breathing, and all the while attempting to relax in the face of a series of precise calibrations of your twisted spine. It's like learning to drive—mirror, signal, manoeuvre, find the biting point, try not to drive into that bus queue. I would say, though you've probably already guessed, I never learned to drive. My lack of spatial awareness became . . . an issue, as the lessons progressed.

She isn't someone from my class. She too totters into podiatry. Judging by the rest of the walking wounded bodies, the clenching and distention, you'd think feet were the last thing they had to worry about. Still, Pilates teaches us everything is connected. As if you needed to be taught that. We're all skeletons in meat pyjamas. Our vascular systems look like the spaghetti of wires beneath your parent's P.C. We're a circuit board made of mince, and I don't need Pilates to tell me that. What next? Breathing is important for your health and should be encouraged? That one's the central plank of the whole exercise.

I'm now alone in the waiting room, waiting. I investigate a painting, stylised figures in a swimming pool. It's nicely painted, good colours, the swimming bodies naïve but charming. I look at the other painting in the waiting room. The title is "The Tree of Understanding". It's a mushroom-shaped tree and you can see, scored into the green oil, pencil-scratched phrases: "I hate war". "Communication". "Love is all you need". I can name, off the top of my head, ten things I need other than love. Shoes, for one. It's a very insensitive position to take outside a podiatry clinic.

I sit down. I look at my phone. I'm facing the very real prospect of a one-to-one session with the instructor. Nowhere to run, nowhere to hide.

An erotic scenario creeps in, the shameful spectre of '90s cable shows, a *Red Shoe Diary* played out on stinking yoga mats. Soft focus, saxophone-accented montages of closed eyes and parted lips, manicured, manly hands sliding over tight-fitting Lycra, and . . . I dismiss it completely. How ridiculous. My back would never take the strain, and nothing says erotic frisson more than a man writhing on the floor in tracksuit bottoms, white and sweaty with pain, as unable to flip himself over as a turtle on its back. I shiver.

My t-shirt for this session, a white and apple-green striped number from Seasalt Cornwall, is rather fetching. On its own. Not with my red and white head sticking out of its collar, like a poorly bandaged stump.

It occurs to me, for the first time, the session might have been cancelled. But they would have told me, surely? I check my phone. It's due to start in one minute. No one has gone in or out in the quarter of an hour. I listen against the door. Nothing appears to be happening inside. But there's a sign on the door telling me there's a "Session in Progress".

I walk down the corridor to the physiotherapy area to knock on their door and see if they know what's going on, and immediately I hear a crowd behind me. Ah, I think, there was a class in the room after all, and that's the sound of the session breaking up. I run back only to discover a lift-load of podiatry people hobbling into the waiting area. No one has come out of the room. I knock on the door again. Nothing. I try the door handle. It rattles in my hand, stubbornly locked.

"Can I help you, pal?" This is a standard greeting in Northern Ireland, often the prelude to a fight, but not this time. It's the janitor. He's helping me.

"Hi," I say, "I'm, er, supposed to have a Pilates class in here."

He doesn't know what Pilates is. But he still wants to help, and frogmarches me back down the gangway to the physiotherapy room, banging on the door.

"I used to have a key. But I don't have a key now," he explains. I don't know what to say to that, so my face does a little dance: some gratitude, a little curiosity, quite a lot of "shit happens". A physio appears at the door. A sleeve of tattoos. Oliver Peoples glasses. A centre parting. He's half my age. The janitor, whose name I never learn, intercedes on my behalf.

"This gentleman was supposed to be doing a Pilates class." He pronounces Pilates carefully, as though the word were hot in his mouth.

"Yeah, it's cancelled," says the boy, blankly. "Didn't you get a message?"

"I did not."

"Ah well," he says, "that's my bad. What's your name?" I tell him my name. It evaporates into the ether. "Really sorry, mate. You should have been told."

"Why was it cancelled?"

"Yeah, it was cancelled."

"Right," I say, "alright." I smile.

"Alright."

I thank the janitor—"No bother, pal"—and go home, spine rigid with annoyance. I'm the least supple I've ever been, a creature of kindling, crackling with every step. My left knee hurts. My right hip hurts. My lower back is like a concrete girdle, powdering at every footfall. My underpants fill with builder's dust.

ME BIG END'S GONE

SUSAN'S MOTHER is visiting. Her pre-Christmas manifestation, as fixed in the calendar as the start of grouse-shooting season or International Men's Day (19th of November, guys). The weather's not looking good, it's December in Northern Ireland, but the Tuesday of the week she's here is nice. It's also the day of my Pilates class. Susan and Vera spend the morning in Belfast city centre, and I spend it typing, like I do every day. My life *does* lack variety. I go for a walk every day, and I go to Pilates once a week and I eat, sleep and type and that, pretty much, is what I do. Seriously, my one regular appointment in the week is doing breathing exercises next to a man farting through his catalogue jeans. I believe de Maupassant had a rather livelier time of it.

The two of them get back with their Christmas gifts, and there's a bit of cold-air bustle in the kitchen and I make them cups of tea, and they plan their afternoon. They're going to drive out to a Garden Centre and potter round the potting sheds. Sounds like some seriously low impact fun, but they like it. So that's what they do, and I return to stare into the baleful eye of the computer screen.

Five minutes later they're back. The car won't start. Amber displays are lighting up the dashboard like fireworks. A flashing sign tells us the airbag won't deploy, though we have no need to deploy the airbag as the car won't start. I go out to look at it, even though we all know I have nothing to offer here. There are strange hieroglyphs sporting beneath the steering wheel. My instinct is to suggest she turn the car off and on again. But we can't turn the car on. That's the problem, in fact.

We go back to the house. It might be the electrics. It might be some sort of unhelpful fail-safe overriding the car's ability to start. We Google stuff. Susan is with the A.A. so we call them, but they refuse to do anything because she's not stranded by a roadside somewhere. We drink coffee in the house and look out the window at the deceased car.

Eventually we call a garage, and they agree to tow it away and fix it. Their estimated time of arrival is "any time in the next six hours", and Susan goes to the kitchen to reheat some parsnip soup she's made for her mother. At once I see a tow-truck pull up outside the house. Blimey, that was quick. It's half two. My Pilates class is at three fifteen. I'm already in my full outfit: trainers, tracksuit bottoms, Bulgakov t-shirt and anorak.

The bloke analyses the situation. It's the battery. The battery's died. He tells Susan not to tow the car back to the garage and give up the car for a couple of days. He can jump-start it; we can take it to his mate's garage and get the battery fitted in the next hour or so. It would be quicker and about a third of the price. I appear at Susan's shoulder, and he instantly addresses all the car talk to me, a man, in sportswear. This is the second time this has happened. The last time the car had a problem the bloke from the A. A. looked over Susan's shoulder to address all his comments to me and, though it was repeatedly pointed out to him that she was the driver, he couldn't stop himself. These men are young. How are they sexist? How are there still sexists? Why does society utterly fail to evolve?

I'm getting caught up in this, but I'm late. Normally the last thing I do is pick up my keys from the tasteful flamenco dancer key hook next to the door but, today, as I was caught up in a flurry of vehicular intrigue on the doorstep, I just slipped through and headed off down the street.

I'd just taken my shoes and socks off when my phone rang. People were still arriving, so I apologised to the Pilates instructor and picked up the call. It was Susan. She was at the garage and Vera had just whispered in her ear, "Did you turn the soup off?" She couldn't remember. She was mildly panicked. The previous night she'd had a dream in which the house had caught fire and now it looked like a self-fulfilling prophesy. She was stuck carless at the garage, could I go home and check on the kitchen?

"I'm sorry," I said to Caoilfhionn, "I have to go!", gathering up my shoes, socks and coat. She looked shocked. "Of course," no doubt imagining car crashes, hands caught in industrial presses, anthrax attacks or hostile action undertaken by persons unknown. I grabbed the door handle and rattled it. It refused to give. I rattled it some more, and it gave, slightly. I was like a mother lifting a car off her child. I'm sure I could have wrenched it off its hinges in my passion.

"There's a button," said Caoilfhionn.

I saw no button.

"On the side, by the door. A button."

She was mad. There was no button. I rattled the door. The creak of splintering wood.

"Where? Where is the button?"

She took my arm and dragged it slowly down. I went with it, and there, finally, was the button. It was hidden by the arm of a treadmill, the obscuring of the button ex-actly calibrated for a person of my height. Only I, of the entire room of people, would not have been able to see that button. Half an inch shorter or taller and it would have been clear as day. It was hidden perfectly only from me. I pressed the button and ran into the waiting room, still holding my anorak, shoes and socks.

"Good luck!" said Caoilfhionn, wondering if she'd ever see me again.

"Thanks," I said, probably grittily. Possibly chewing on a matchstick.

I sat down in the chair in the waiting room. I'm in a hurry but my socks are new and stiff and it's taking a long time to bend them over my toes. When the socks were finally on, I started the lengthy process of knotting the incredibly long laces on my trainers. Why are laces on sports shoes longer than your arms? I was still looping and pulling, when Caoilfhionn looked out the door again, presumably looking for Eddie (or Freddie) who hadn't turned up yet and saw me still sat in a chair in the wait-ing room, idly toying with my shoelaces, while cars piled up on the A320 and Godzilla picked his teeth with a chair leg. Her face blared, "Oh, an emergency, is it?"

Nevertheless, once shod, I ran down those stairs two at a time and was out into the cool air of the afternoon, speeding into traffic, and over to the bus stop. Which was no longer there. They'd moved the bus stop.

Okay.

I continued running, reasoning there must be a bus stop somewhere on this road. If they don't stop, buses lose quite a bit of their practical use. Though I doubt, even then, they'd run on time in Belfast.

I sped up the road and could see the familiar profile of the Glider Halt, just as the bus sped past me. Perfect. No, wait. It's stopping. I *can* get this bus. I wedged my foot in the doors just as they were beginning to close, and they snapped back. I sat down, pretending not to hyperventilate in my non-breathing plastic coat, arms a slick of sweat. Phew. I'd be back in about fifteen minutes, barring accidents.

Keys.

I had no keys.

Shitshitshitshitshit.

For the first time ever, I'd come out without my keys.

Fuck a cow!

I rang Susan.

"Hi, I'm on the bus. I should be back in around fifteen minutes. But here's the thing, I don't have my keys."

"Oh."

"But I can go round the back of the house. The door's glass and it's directly opposite the cooker. So, I can at least see whether the hob's on, or the kitchen's . . . on fire . . ."

I remembered her nightmare.

"The hob may not even *be* on. But if it is I can easily assess the damage."

"I've sent mum with the keys in a taxi," she said, "she should be there soon. Sorry for getting you out of Pilates."

"That doesn't matter. You just relax. Everything's going to be fine. I'll be home soon, and I'll be able to assess the situation. And your mum will be able to get me in the house. It'll all be fine, I promise."

And I meant it. But equally, I thought of the peculiar set of circumstances that saw the three of us split up over the city: Susan at a garage she'd never heard of an hour ago. Vera, speeding, key in hand, across a city she barely knew. Me, now staring through the condensation on my back door window at a saucepan that was doing absolutely nothing at all. The hob *was* on—it hadn't been a complete farce—but I could tell by the pointers on the knobs the soup was on gas mark one or two. Also, as it's a ceramic hob there's no naked flame. There was no steam coming off the soup, nothing spattering, no smoke, no smell. The pan hadn't burnt out or warped. I rubbed my breath away again and looked at an entirely undynamic pan of soup sitting on a hob. I went round the front to wait for Vera.

When we got in the house the smell was surprisingly delicious. I turned off the hob—it was on "two"—and looked at the soup. It was, as Vera succinctly put it, "thick as shite on a blanket", but it hadn't burned onto the pan and I stuck it in the bin, washed down the pot and the hob and everything was fine. Horror averted.

Susan returned. The car was fixed. The good weather was wasted but, as I pointed out, waiting to hear the amount of money necessary to make the car work would be even more depressing in the rain.

And the upshot of it is Susan felt so bad about my missing my class, she's agreed to do a Pilates class with me in the New Year. We shall have cores of iron.

I have no idea what I'm going to tell my shaken Pilates instructor next week, as she's bound to ask if everything is okay.

"Yeah, I had to duck out of class to view a saucepan full of soup through my kitchen window."

She may doubt my commitment.

A Cuckoo in the Nest
of Vipers

───────◆───────

THERE'S A SMALL GLASS SCREEN in the waiting room. I've never noticed it before. It's in the Pepsi colours, has a swoosh, and bears the legend "Fusion". There's a clock on it, but nothing changes on the screen but the time. I have no idea what it's for. The screen is about three inches by four and it's built into the wall. It must have always been there, but for over a month I've missed it each time I've been in this room. What a mystery. I'd ask someone, but there's no one to ask. I'm alone in the waiting room, pathologically early once again.

It's nowhere near the door of the podiatry centre. It's right in the middle of the wall. It's buried alive in the brickwork, like Fortunato in *The Cask of Amontillado*—Fusionato—and I stare at it, fearful of letting my gaze drift, and it flashing some sudden change in my peripheral vision, a winking tell-all LED display betraying its function.

I get so obsessed with it I don't notice the waiting room filling up, and I'm shocked back into the crowded room when a woman sits down next to me and says hello. We have a brief, friendly conversation. There's the usual frisson when she hears my accent for the first time. This has happened for a decade, ever since I moved to Northern Ireland. Older people wonder why someone with an English accent would be living anywhere near them, as we're all chinless millionaires in tweeds, our soft hands in their pockets. And here I am, wet southern burr, with a bristly chin, sportswear and soaking up limited NHS resources. I'm something they've not imagined before. Luckily, it's Christmas, so we can both talk about how the nights are drawing in and how we're having a quiet one this year.

Some consternation. The door opens and we're beckoned into the Pilates room by a woman *who isn't Caoilfhionn*. As she welcomes us in, we are ticked off a list, but *no stickers with our names are forthcoming*. What fresh hell is this?

This new woman—whose name I don't catch—is older than Caoilfhionn and has a schoolmarmish quality. She wants to see how well we're getting on. Is she Caoilfhionn's boss? Is she checking up on her? I feel a sudden loyalty to my yoga teacher, whom I haven't properly seen for three weeks. I'm very loyal, very fast. I decide I will do my very best. There's about half the class left: five of us, but we're all still expecting Eddie, who is fifteen minutes late every week and knocks on the door at half past. He takes off his anorak and kicks off his shoes and he's good to go. He's wearing a shirt and sweater and jeans. He's about to enter child pose dressed in his gardening clothes.

We start the session doing balance exercises standing up. I hate balance exercises. As I've mentioned previously, my legs are different sizes and shapes, and my left leg, stiff and unyielding, is the grunt leg, doing most of the work. My right—curling and demure—is largely decorative, a rusted fitting. It's used mostly as a kind of kickstand. So, I have balance issues.

Like Caoilfhionn, this new instructor is a big fan of the "silly daddy" school of instruction. "That's it, girls, very good. Come on boys, the girls are leaving you behind, here. I don't know . . ." Is she appealing to my masculine competitive nature? Is standing on one leg a major player in the eternal battle of the sexes? Are we being motivated along gender lines? It doesn't work on me—I can't answer for Freddie and Eddie. I cannot seem to balance on either leg, wobbling and staggering, as she strolls between us, stern as Debbie Allen's character in *Fame*, and right here is where we start paying—in sweat. And bruised egos.

And no, I'm not explaining that reference. I know it was a long time ago, but everyone should have a basic working knowledge of *Fame*. Look it up. You have a phone in your hand. It'll take a second. I'm sick of spoon-feeding you people. God.

Once we hit the floor it's a different matter. I've been doing my exercises. My core's as hot as the centre of the earth's. I allow myself a grim smile, the sort of smile Batman would give if called upon to perform a single leg bridge. And you never know when that might come in handy in his unrelenting fight against crime. I bet he spends hours on his back in the Batcave, maintaining a stable pelvis and spine while Alfred reminds him to breathe.

My prowess is noted. I'm made an example of. "Very good, John, is it?" It is John, yes. And I am very good. I'm a good boy.

After the session, and after I've carefully tied my shoelaces and put on my anorak (mittens sadly not dangling from the sleeves) I bounce up to teacher while she's talking to her trainee.

"Thanks for that," I say, "great session."

This is not the sort of thing I would normally say, but I'm aware she's not been getting the sort of upbeat responses she might have expected in week five of a six-week course. The class has halved since it started, and some of my classmates are still unwilling to do basic moves for reasons more mental than physical (I'm speculating—I'm not qualified to give a medical diagnosis—my theories are based on suspicion and un-kindness) and it can't be easy coming into a class at week five, regardless.

"Thanks," she says, frostily. "What's wrong with your leg?"

"Oh, I broke it, broke my knee a while ago. It didn't heal properly. It's a bit shorter than the other one, and it tends to get a bit stiff after physical exercise. But that was great."

She looks me up and down.

"You should have told me at the start of the session. I mean, why *wouldn't* you?"

"I dunno."

"Did you tell Keelfon?"

"Caoilfhionn."

"Did you tell her? At the start of the first session—does she know about this?"

"No, well . . . no, it didn't really come up."

"It didn't come up after five weeks?"

"Well, I wasn't here last week . . . I left some soup on . . ."

There's a moment.

"Okay, I'll be off. Great session. Bye."

And I'm out the door.

What the hell happened there? Have I landed Caoilfhionn in the shit? That woman had total "Undercover Boss" vibes. Did she even *give* a name at the start? I acquitted myself well in the class—barring the balance issues—I'm an apt student, a credit to my instructor. At least I dress for the gig, Eddie. I hadn't let Caoilfhionn down until right at the end. And all because I wanted to be nice to the newbie . . .

I resolve once again to never be friendly to anyone. It leads to disaster. My moist handshake flapping into your general vicinity, and the airing of my ceremonial teeth, might as well be the opening of the seventh seal. Frosty aloofness is always the safest path. Sure, I'll die alone and unloved but think of the damage limitation. Once again, I feel like Batman and *his* bad back, keeping lonely vigil over the city, high up on my rooftop eyrie, always observing but sworn never to interfere, unless it's to punch petty criminals in the face.

Sure, I'm a billionaire, I could be funding a drugs pro-gramme and rebuilding the slum areas of Gotham. But no, I swore to punch criminals in the face at my parents' graveside, and now I fight crime one busted nose-bridge at a time.

Besides, I'm so awkward, socially.

I feel bad. Maybe I should have told Caoilfhionn about the broken knee. It's kind of a big deal. Maybe I should tell *you* about it . . .

THE KNEEBONE'S CONNECTED TO THE . . . WELL, *NOTHING* NOW . . .

———————

THIS WAS A LONG TIME AGO, when the world was young and so was I, nearly. The year was 2002 and I'd survived the 20th Century in one piece, unless you count all the standard childhood trauma.

I had dark hair, long black eyelashes and could still wear vintage clothing because a) it was fashionable b) I was largely the same shape as people from the seventies who'd grown up on the ration. I was living in London, I had a job and a girlfriend, whom I was helping to move into her new flat. It was all so intoxicatingly grown up. I was also limping and wearing borrowed shoes.

Those last two things are important. I was limping because I'd broken my ankle dancing with my friend Ange at a New Year's Eve party. We'd been grooving to "Space Age Bachelor Pad Music," as was the style at the time, my foot slipped on a spillage, and down I went, taking Ange with me and somehow, in this sudden smackdown from gravity, my ankle snapped in two. It hurt. Even through the fog of booze, the ankle was very sore and no longer functioning in a traditional manner. I wouldn't be walking this one off.

I was picked up by other partygoers and taken into a bedroom. While I was lying on my back, my foot elevated and as purple and swollen as a drunken bishop, an energetic Welshman named Crocker stumbled into the room, saw me stretched out in front of the crowd like I was at my own wake, and decided it would be very funny to climb on and *ride me like a bucking bronco*. Eventually, the wall of shocked faces reacting to this delightful prank penetrated his boozy haze, Crocker had a moment of doubt and dismounted. I lay there for the rest of the night while the party raged on about me, desperately willing my ankle to be sprained.

The next morning my foot was so enormous and grey an Edwardian might have attempted to store umbrellas in it, and I thought it best to go to A&E. I phoned a taxi.

It was a cold, bright New Year's Day and there was a ground frost. At the hospital I paid the taxi driver and hopped out of the car. The air was chill on my naked toes. Hmm. It *was* quite a big carpark, and the driver had made little effort to leave me close to the building. The hospital entrance was a hive of activity. There were people smoking on the forecourt, most of them in night attire, some attached to drips taller than standard lamps.

I would have to hop across the carpark. I turned to the driver, but he was showily doing something else, anything else, rather than meet my gaze. I'd already paid him, after all.

Cheers.

I did well. I hopped halfway across the forecourt before going down, but down I did go, hitting the gravel hard and pushing the air out of my lungs, my head hitting the tarmac with a crack. I lay on my back, hoping to relearn the skill of drawing air into my body, when I heard a car starting. I can still see, in my mind's eye, the passivity of the taxi driver reversing out of my eye-line. Mirror, signal, man overboard. The prick.

People talk about the coldness of the big city, the indifference of the urban population, the portcullis-down insularity of the modern metropolitan community. I've never found this. Cities are just villages, the connective tissue invisible and underground. There are kind, decent people who will care for you everywhere. But not this taxi driver, not this prick. This prick was a prick.

Far more typical were the gaggle of elderly women, some of whom were attached to drips, all of whom had fags in their mouths, who rushed towards me and attempted to get me to my feet and, when they succeeded, took me, hopping and barely breathing, into the hospital, where a security guard immediately attempted to throw them all out again for smoking.

"It's alright," I gasped, like wheezing royalty, "they're with me!"

Somehow that worked, and they were allowed to escort me into A&E. Nice people. They're probably all dead now.

I'd broken my ankle. They operated on my foot, placed pins and screws in it, and plastered it up. It was only the second time I'd ever broken a bone. I was about to break a lot of them.

The first bone I'd broken—I'm giving myself too much credit here, *I* didn't break it—was a decade before, when I'd been attacked by a gang of thugs coming home from a club in Basingstoke. They knocked me out, and I woke up in a hedge with a broken arm. Unprovoked physical assaults are a staple of small-town living. I'm a writer. I like stories. I like cause and effect, payoffs. But you don't get a lot of narrative clarity with a random punch to the side of the head, or someone you've never met before attempting to strangle you in a petrol station.

But the busted ankle did make sense. I could hobble about on my big, white foot, being careful not to get it soggy in the bath, and it was fine. It didn't hurt. It didn't even impact on my social life, greatly. There were no complications. It healed.

A few months later, my girlfriend bought a flat, and I thought I'd help her move. At which point the complications crowded in.

An awful lot of booze has flowed under the bridge in the past twenty years, and my once steel-trap brain is more rust than metal. So, I asked my then girlfriend, Chloe, if she could remember what happened, and maybe we could collaborate on a sort of Cubist approach to my history of bone-splintering. It turns out her memory's almost as bad as mine. At this point your narrator becomes even more unreliable than usual.

One of the things I *do* remember about being in hospital throughout the summer of 2002, is writing nothing down. Nowadays, if I squirt toothpaste in my eye or have a bad shave, there's a thousand-word essay about it. But I wrote nothing then. I had a typewriter in the hospital at one point (did I? Did I really?) and I always had pens and paper, but I ne'er writ a line.

I read. I listened to *On the Town with The League of Gentlemen* on cassette over and over because I *really* needed a laugh. But I recorded none of my experiences. There are, however, things I recall vividly, and one of them is I was wearing someone else's shoes the day I helped Chloe move flat. Why? Chloe is little help here:

Chloe: *"I don't think you favoured trainers at the time (you fool!), and I felt you would need a plimsoll for grip/feeling sporty and spry. Ski boots or perhaps a full body cast might have been a better idea."* She's hilarious. *"Your options would have been Pete, Stew or Anthony. And there's no reason why I would retain any information about the size of their feet in relation to yours."*

She doth protest too much. Pete, Stew and Anthony were my flatmates at the time, and there's no way I would have borrowed their footwear—we didn't have a shoe-swapping level of intimacy—but there is a name ghosting into my brain: Paul Shevlane. Paul was a man from work. Why would I have borrowed his footwear? I still recoil in horror from the ick of a damp bowling shoe. But in those days, I only ever had one pair of shoes at a time, and I suppose my reasoning was: this is dirty work, I'd much rather ruin the shoes of a bloke from work than my own. How I convinced him to lend me his shoes is another matter. Was there a trade-off? Did he get the shoes back? So many questions. If you're reading this, Paul, do let me know . . .

So, I was wearing peculiar, alien shoes, moulded to the feet of another man. I had a mending ankle and clumsy shoes, perfect for spending an entire day going up and down strange stairs. What could go wrong?

I'd been taking things up to Chloe's second floor flat and removing the junk, and I remember the fateful load with crystal clarity. It was a cardboard box filled with aluminium stair rods. They were light but long, the box big enough to obscure my feet. As I flapped down the staircase in my boat-sized clown shoes, there was a moment and the world tilted one way, the stair rods the other, and I hit the wall, knee first.

I'm unable to account for what happened. I only fell a couple of steps. The stairs were carpeted, the load was light. So later, as I sat in my pants in a hospital room and listened to junior doctors whooping with incredulity and delight as they examined my X-rays on the lightbox outside, I was surprised by the interest.

"Come and look at this!" they said to passersby, "This is fucking amazing!"

You never want to hear a doctor telling strangers a part of your anatomy is amazing. Even if it's just graffiti in the staff toilets. Surely, it's a breach of the Hippocratic oath?

I'd sustained a spiral fracture in my right leg. They happen when the bone is broken in a twisting motion— say if you're trying to hang on to your precious cargo of stair rods as you start to tumble. The fracture-line resembles a corkscrew, and mine was a textbook spiral fracture. Literally as, I was subsequently informed, my X-Ray had been used in medical textbooks as an example of when spiral fractures *really go for it*.

My right tibia was published twenty years before the rest of me.

Spiral fractures may be referred to as *complete fractures* because the line of the break goes all the way through the bone. They're rare, because they're caused by serious accidents most people don't experience—like clinging to a paper-light cardboard box as you trip down three steps in borrowed footwear—spiral fractures are much less common than other kinds of breaks.

None of this was going through my mind, however, as I lay at the foot of the stairs in the shared hallway of Chloe's new flat, surrounded by pizza menus, taxi flyers, and several lengths of aluminium piping. I was focused on the white heat of pain, eclipsing anything I'd experienced before, that was suddenly visited on my right knee, where the slightest movement sent shivers of electric agony snaking through my body, as my face drained, my teeth ground, my eyes clamped shut. I also thought that this was probably the end of my usefulness as a removal man.

Chloe found me, pale and uncommunicative beyond grunts, and with her usual presence of mind, gathered as orderlies the manager of the shop next door and one of the friendly drug dealers who worked from our doorstep. Coldharbour Lane was a vibrant and buzzing place, and I was very glad of the available manpower.

The two men lifted me up and bundled me into a car. Whose car? I don't think Chloe had a car at that point, though maybe she did. The store manager's car? The drug dealer didn't seem the type to have a car, he was quite junior, so the store manager seems the most likely candidate. I don't recall, because all I have are fragmentary images for much of the rest of the day, joggled, sudden pictures, framed by the white static of excruciating pain. I'm in a hospital. I'm on a gurney. I've been given something for the pain, it makes me manic, I lash out and cry, and I echo through the grey corridors as I'm wheeled from place to place on my trolley, arms flapping over the sides, babbling.

Dignified, I am not.

At some point Chloe phones my parents and then, presumably, goes home to continue moving house on her own. Sorry Chloe.

Chloe: *"I remember driving you to King's, getting caught up in a weird bit of one-way/no-left-turn madness, which meant that while we were moments from A&E, it took way longer than it needed to. And I kept having to do stressy 3-point turns, while you sweated, grey-faced and agonised next to me.*

"I have an idea that I was booked onto a team-building event the following week and had to say I couldn't go. It was canoeing at Symond's Yat. I think a Dim View was formed of my commitment to The Team, which endured."

Great. Now I'm jeopardising her career. No good deed goes unpunished. The thing is, helping her move was totally out of character. I was then, and now, self-involved, shiftless and idle. This was supposed to be me turning over a new leaf. Being a proper boyfriend. A hearty, sensible chap with a pension and ambition, the type of guy who bought his jeans from The Gap. Instead, I had the grey skin of a dolphin caught in a tuna trawler's keep-net and was forcing her to navigate South London traffic.

Still, canoeing at Symond's Yat with a load of red-faced wine experts—*Never Mind the Rowlocks—Here's the*

Six Pissheads—sounds like something nobody should ever have to do. And we have established that she had a car, so it's all coming together now.

The hospital she takes me to is Kings College Hospital, situated a handy half mile away from the flat. It's a teaching hospital and major trauma centre, which was also handy. But it's on its last legs at this point. Next to it is a brand-new shiny version of the hospital, gleaming and white and focused on a pristine future. It cost £50,000,000 and it's not opening for another month. It's now the largest liver transplant centre in Europe, which I imagine is very convenient for the lively local population.

But it's not where I'm headed.

I'm rumbling through the corridors of the 1909 version. It's the site of the UK's second ever telephone installation, a hospital that generated its own power through diesel, that tended to the sick and dying of both World Wars. It's the birthplace, in 1947, of the current Queen, Camilla, and it was where Mad Frankie Fraser died. I mean, I love it for its history. If those walls could talk, they'd probably scream in agony. It's solid, stony, echoey, venerable. But it's not in great shape in 2002. There's a smell of piss. There's dirt. The toilet doors have been kicked lockless. People with broken legs are handcuffed to police officers in the corridors.

As I listen to the junior doctors laughing it up at my picture-perfect fracture, I'm sitting on a bench in my pants, half hidden by a curtain. Almost unimaginably, I'm sharing this small room with a weeping teenage girl and her mother. I don't know what news they've been given but it's not good, and I don't want to compound the injury by flashing my genitals at them in the middle of a crisis. I can't see it helping—they're not *that* funny. I can't move my leg, but I can awkwardly shift the curtain, though my mangled limb's still peeping out, as though I'm terrible at hide and seek.

At some point I have an operation. In the theatre. Not in the room I'm sharing with the weepy teen.

After that I'm returned to a ward. It's public ward full of old men with faces as wrinkled and yellow as winter apples, some of whom cry out in the night, some of whom make no noise at all. They barely move, their xylophone chests fluttering, the hard, silent breathing a constant effort, their blue lips wet, stretched white where they meet the pressure of remaining teeth.

For the first nine days on the ward, I'm unable to move my bowel. They feed me. I eat some of it. Nothing comes out.

Next to me is an African pastor in exciting pyjamas. He has one of those cages around his lower leg. It looks like a Medieval torture device, an iron maiden hugging your shin like an amorous puppy. He's not popular on the ward. Every night members of his congregation process into the room, their high-end glamour contrasting badly with the generally moribund surroundings. They pray and sing for an hour at high volume. Then all but one of them leaves in a solemn and dignified train, while the straggler, whom I assume is the Pastor's wife, shuts the curtains around the bed and gives him noisy, mercifully brief hand relief. A couple of minutes elapse, she emerges, perfectly composed, and draws back the curtains again, to reveal him sat up on his cushions, smiling. Night after night. Like I say, he wasn't popular.

I have a catheter fitted. It's rather like having a cocktail umbrella introduced to your urethra. Eyes water. I'd say having it put in was one of the most humiliating and uncomfortable experiences of my life, a life that wasn't exactly shy of discomfort and humiliation, but taking it out again was much, much worse. I sprinkled as I tinkled for a good year after. It didn't just snap back.

On day nine, I finally asked the nurses what I could do about my constipation. They assured me it was common in cases of shock and trauma. I would have thought the opposite was true and wondered why I was having to ask them about not pooing for over a week. Surely that's the sort of thing nurses should be flagging up. It's, like, medical. But, you know, they're busy people.

They bring me a commode, close the curtains, and present me with a couple of suppositories. I stare blankly at them. They explain how to use them, efficiently, and without recourse to a Swanee whistle. In many ways, I'm an innocent—unsophisticated and naïve—so when I tell you until this point my bottom had been one-way traffic only, you'll not be surprised. Nevertheless, I'd been given a task by a medical professional, and I wouldn't shrink from it. I manoeuvred myself over the commode, removed my shorts and gingerly brushed the appropriate area with the pill, the gentlest kiss of capsule on anus.

Krakatoa.

Krapatoa, in fact.

A weeks' worth was disgorged in a split-second, silently and surprisingly. Oh, I said, oh, oh, oh, oh, oh, oh. I imagine my face was a picture. A picture of Kenneth Williams. I cleaned myself up, quietly marvelling at broke-bum mountain, and realising that I now had to serve up this heap-spoon helping to one of the nurses. A nurse whom I would see every day. She wouldn't care, of course. But I would. The shame lurched in the pit of my

THE KNEEBONE'S CONNECTED TO THE . . .

stomach. Hospitals are cathedrals of humiliation. You arrive weak, vulnerable and helpless, and you remain in that condition, the dignity stripped from you. You are unpeeled. You have no secrets; you have no other life. You are a naked animal in pain. You are the patient.

I tried to dress the poo in the bowl with a discreet turban of toilet paper. The nurse came and drew back the curtains and took it away, her face impassive, unreadable. The Pastor looked at me with very legible disdain, the cheeky fucker. I knew what went on behind his curtains. We all did. Lucky prick.

I develop MRSA on the ward. That's methicillin-resistant staphylococcus aureus, to you. It's a bacterium that usually lives harmlessly on the skin, but on contact with a wound—a darling little gateway to your insides—it becomes problematic. Because of the nature of my injury, I was likely looking at osteomyelitis, a serious infection that sees the bone marrow infected. I didn't know any of this. I just knew it was a new thing that was in the newspapers that year—MRSA was the only topic of conversation in society parties that summer—and then, suddenly, I was off the ward and into a hospice room on my own. This was when they started to open the wound to clean it out on a regular basis. I was wheeled through the hospital on a gurney to have my wound opened and washed out every couple of days.

It was also when they stopped remembering to feed me. It was a hospice room, and the usual occupants were in comas and fed on drips. I listened out for the breakfast trolley as it rolled past—I was always awake, it was summer, it was hot, the curtains in the room were like tracing paper—and banged on the door with my crutch to try and get the orderly to stop. When they did remember to feed me, the food was not great. Who puts gravy on a quiche? Guys, come on. By the time I was out of the hospital I'd lost three stone.

They also didn't clear up my piss bottles. I'm not sure why. It was, as I say, a hot summer and the smell of urine must have been . . . noisome. My little leper's tent was right next to the nurse's reception area and must have stank. But still no one came, as the piss evaporated in the bottle, a gift to the air conditioning. The demon's portion.

At a remove of twenty years all of this seems astonishing. At the time Chloe wrote a strongly worded letter to the hospital—sadly lost to the rigours of another house move—motivated by her rage. I was apparently extraordinarily fatalistic and stoic about the whole thing. But I didn't feel particularly stoic about it. By about the sixth week—the halfway point, as it turned out—I thought I was losing my mind.

Around this time my boss visited me, prompted one assumes, by Human Resources, who must have noticed I was getting paid for malingering in hospital. The look on his face as he saw me on my narrow bed in my little plastic room, a stone skinnier, and wearing a Yosemite Sam beard. The dye in my hair was growing out, and the black hovered over the white at my hairline like an upturned Guinness. I was sat on the bed in t-shirt and boxer shorts, my balls making regular bids for freedom, and surrounded by vases of piss like votive offerings placed around the bed; a household shrine designed by Alejandro Jodrowsky.

I was in tears of gratitude just to see a new face and smiling sadly through the scrub of my beard. He didn't get very far through his questionnaire without scoring a fat black line through it. Giving me a very firm handshake, he told me to take all the time I needed, he'd square it all, then he left in haste. If he could have pressed a handkerchief to his mouth to staunch my stench without causing offence, he would have done so. And I'd have been fine with it—I was well beyond taking offence.

Chloe: *"I started getting you those wraps from the Sun and Doves,* (a pub on nearby Coldharbour Lane) *but they had 'too much flavour', so I'd bring you something down from home after I got back from work. Once they twigged you were effectively being starved, they gave you these hyper-nutritional drinks they give to malnourished elderly people.*

"You were still emaciated when you finally got home, which I was shamelessly pro, a deeply unhelpful sentiment, I can't help thinking now. Sorry about that."

(You ought to be ashamed of yourself.)

"And then there was a two-bedded bay with a fellow-MRSA contaminant for a spell. I can't remember if that was before or after they applied the charcoal filter pump thing to your leg, to draw the oomska out (which in my memory took place in the single isolation room). And there were trips to theatre to wash the wound out, and blood transfusions."

I'd forgotten about the blood transfusions.

I had so many blood transfusions I ran out of viable veins, so I had yet another operation to insert a Hickman line. A Hickman line is a central catheter placed on the right side of your chest wall. It ends in a large vein just above your heart. The veins in my arms were rubbish at the best of times, and by that point my forearms resembled scabby flutes, so they wheeled me off again. I didn't mind at all. The hospital was so incredibly boring, that an operation was like a day out. They wheel you in, there's some perfunctory chat, they apply a mask to your face and advise you to count backwards from ten, there are chilly gulps of gas and then a slow freefall into black velvet oblivion. You can see why people get into drugs. The cool bliss of nullification, the emptying out into the infinite. It's better than banging on your window with a stick for some bran flakes.

The Hickman Line operation was not like this—they don't knock you out. They numb your chest, so you don't feel them rummaging about inside you like they're looking for a purse in a handbag. But you *do* feel it. You don't feel the pain, but your body moves, you can feel the movement. It tightens your skin. Pulls on your muscles. Equally, so you can't see the big hole they're digging in your chest, they place a papery blue cloth over your face, like the cone the dog wears to stop him chewing on his stitches. This is not only claustrophobic, but it does not, in any way, muffle the chat of the surgeons operating on you. The subject of the conversation was not me, and I was not involved in the conversation, despite being present. It was the bland chatter of two butchers discussing their busy weekends while jointing a chicken. After this dehumanising ordeal, I was happy to get back to my boiling, piss-stinking cupboard for once.

A junior doctor took pity on me. He told me one day, "You're not like the other patients on the ward, Mr Higgins." He was right—I wasn't on the ward. I think he was implying I was cleverer than the other people, and my brilliant mind was suffering more, but as he then prescribed me a daily can of Guinness, maybe he just thought I was a bigger lush than they were. Anyway, it was an act of kindness, and I wept like a child, which neither of us enjoyed.

Chloe: *"I do remember being told the rationale for the charcoal filter pump was to avoid the risk of infection spreading into the bone. The implication being that this would be bad. I remember researching all manner of innovative treatments for MRSA, including calcium pellets drenched in tea-tree oil. The medics looked at me like I'd lost my mind after I brought that up.*

"It was such a weird plunge into a deeply odd world. Prior to that, I'd always been the person in the centre of some awful medical crisis, and because you're always off your tits on drugs, and what have you, you just sort of surrender yourself to the experience.

"I feel like being alongside and having to be supportive is harder at the time. Clearly, once the crisis had passed, I could revert to normal life. You were left with all the long-term consequences."

Yes, but I'm getting a book out of it so it's not all bad.

There were a lot of terrible moments from this complicated and far-reaching event. Things that were my fault (getting drunk and falling over on crutches, breaking my wrist), things that weren't (spending twelve hours in A&E, because the pseudomonas infecting the plate in my leg had erupted into a volcano of green pus in the toilets at work) and things that were just the ordinary outcome of what happened to me (self-consciously growing meat in the hole in my leg—you could see the bone—because the nurse intimated it would go badly for me if I didn't. I believed this to have been a manifestation of a low-level superpower. Call me The Mince Master.

Chloe mainly remembers she'd made some really good bacon sandwiches, just before the nurse arrived to give me the all-clear, and her bad timing spoiled them. Fair enough. She did make amazing bacon sandwiches.

Chloe: *"I remember you calling from work to say you had a lump on your leg around 11am that day. You didn't want to go to A&E, as you'd only been back at work very briefly by that point (late September, maybe). So, you stayed until the end of the day. It was a Friday. Friday night in A&E. Jesus.*

"I think I went down to yours to collect some roquefort and a knife, for sustenance. At least we had quality A&E snacks."

I'm glad we took a knife to A&E. It was pretty rough. We were there from five-thirty in the evening to five-thirty in the morning, by which point we were both so delirious we were giggling. At about one in the morning, I saw a doctor who—as I recall—prodded the green mush in my leg with his pen! We then waited another few hours, until another doctor told us we might as well go home and we did, hysterical and hobbling into daybreak. I genuinely don't remember how my leg was cured from spewing green pus. But it must have done, because it hasn't happened recently.

There was one final meeting about my shattered leg I still shiver to recall.

I'd been out of the hospital for a while. My work was sending a car for me every day which was, in hindsight, remarkable. I was a lowly figure in the office, and fantastically bad at my job. I wasn't lazy, just incredibly unsuited to office work. I'd managed to avoid computers for the first twenty-five years of my life—I eschewed arcade games, I cold-shouldered *Horace Goes Skiing*, I'd taken little interest in *Tekken*, my *Game and Watch* were two separate things. Even after I'd got my first office job, for an insurance company which had its own internal messaging system—this was before email—I found workarounds, because I didn't competently know how to press "send". I'd write the messages down and casually walk them round the building, as though I were just passing through, and thought I'd pass on the message as I was there. No one ever knew. Or if they did know, no one ever fired me, which is just as good. Yes, it's odd—as I type this into my laptop, with one finger, admittedly, flitting between screens I can dazzle on various social media forums— there was a time where I would have to deliver my witticisms, puffing and sweating, by hand.

I was so fit in those days.

But when they sent the car to take me to work, I was not fit, hobbling down the stairs on my crutches, almost bowled over by my flatmates, who worked in the same office, and were eager to get to the car and listen to *Talk Sport* as we beetled through rush-hour traffic.

I was pleased there was some normality in my life. I went to work. I came home. I forget how I foraged for food, but I must have done, as I'm still alive.

The district nurse no longer visited, and the outpatient appointments were drying up. The healing would be up to me now.

But I did have one more out-of-office appointment and, as I'm a good boy, I bowled up to the hospital. I was quite young at the time, barely thirty, but I remember thinking the doctor who greeted me looked a little on the youthful side. Sandy hair, freckles, embarrassed-looking rosy cheeks. He was the dead-spit of Kevin's older brother in *The Wonder Years*. It wasn't reassuring.

"Mr Higgins," said Dougie Hauser, "I've been reading your notes."

"Okay."

I'd never seen him before in my life. What happened to the other doctors I'd seen, the ones who shaved? Why was this mewling pup going through my notes, tracing his finger under them, mouthing the words? Would there be milk sick and rusk crumbs smeared onto them when he returned them to the filing cabinet he could barely reach?

He was young, is, I guess, what I'm trying to say. Long white coat, short trousers.

"Mr Higgins," he said, again, "I've been reading your notes."

"Okay."

"It's good news, Mr Higgins."

"Okay."

"It looks as though you're going to be able to keep your leg."

"Oka . . . WHAT?"

What happened next was unfair. I experienced a series of emotions but, as realisation dawned, they were nothing compared to the doctor's. Once he realised that nobody, but nobody, had ever intimated the possibility that I might *actually lose my leg*, an unspoken secret buried deep in the notes, and one he had just guilelessly revealed directly to my startled face, he went into meltdown. His eyes grew wide and watered, the colour drained from his rosy face. I may have forced a sudden puberty on him. I was the man who broke his voice.

My brain neatly compartmentalised the situation. On the one hand I was watching this small boy deliquesce in front of me with cool disdain. Oh dear, I thought, I don't suppose he's had to deliver good news that's this bad before. The other half of my brain was melting like toasted cheese on a grill. THEY WERE GOING TO CUT MY LEG OFF! THEY WERE GOING TO CUT MY FUCKING LEG OFF! THEY WERE GOING TO CUT MY FUCKING LEG OFF AND THEY NEVER EVEN TOLD ME. YOU'D THINK THAT SORT OF THING WOULD HAVE COME UP IN CONVERSATION.

"Looking through a winter sports brochure, Mr Higgins? Oh, you're going skiing? Tell me, have you ever thought about snowboarding? I'll tell you for why . . ."

"Two slippers, Mr Higgins? A trifle indulgent, don't you think . . .?"

"Best foot forward, Mr Higgins? That's the spirit. After all, it's not like you get to *pick* your best foot, is it? Ha ha ha."

I thought of the man with one leg who'd emerged from the lockless toilet back in the hospital, wreathed in cigarette smoke. I thought of the slow, obscene wink he gave me. I thought of *Treasure Island*, because my knowledge of monopods was not great. I thought of Douglas Bader but dismissed him as he had no legs at all. They'd put me in the Paralympics, surely? Isn't it like National Service? Then I'd be on *Strictly Come Dancing* bouncing on a carbon-fibre blade, and being patronised by a wet-eyed Shirley Ballas, who'd stand and applaud my every dance, and vote me off before Movies week. That was my unspoken future, hidden from me, but crawling, with a life of its own, in the spidery hand of my doctor, until this junior buffoon had exorcised it.

"What do you mean I'm going to keep my leg?"

"I thought you'd been told . . ."

"Yes, you would bloody well think I'd have been told. No one ever mentioned I was going to lose my leg."

"But you're not," he squeaked. "It's good news."

"Yes, you keep saying that."

He dropped the notes at that point. And spent a few minutes picking them up and returning them to some semblance of order which, I thought at the time was further evidence of his youthful idiocy, but now realise was a sophisticated piece of misdirection. The fucker should have been in the Magic Circle. By the time he'd collected the various bits of foolscap and packed them back into his ring binder, I was sitting down, gently decompressing, and accepting that I was now unlikely to lose a leg I had not realised I was in danger of losing. He too had regained some composure, and we sat in the café—where all this had taken place—and had a few moments perfunctory conversation about the care and upkeep of my now peculiar leg, as though it were an exotic pet I was charged with caring for. Don't get it wet. Don't feed it after midnight.

And I hobbled home.

And that was sort of it.

I wonder if Chloe remembers anything else.

Chloe: *"I remember your mum and dad coming to visit you, and your dad very carefully removed all the extant screws and rawl plugs from the walls, and then loaned me his ratchet screwdriver and a special piece of ply for ongoing use when I took the kitchen down.*

"He also helped me build the kitchen units and hang the wall cabinets. I still have the ratchet screwdriver I bought because I was

so impressed with its brilliance. It's the same model he had. Your dad was the platonic ideal of Dad."

Ah, she remembers my dad helping her with the DIY, while I was laid up in hospital. Fair enough. My dad was good at that sort of thing. He was very careful, very patient, a real measure twice, cut once merchant. Me falling down the stairs and shattering my knee was a real boon to her interior-design ambitions, as I would have been terrible at assembling cabinets. He was careful, precise and calm. A textbook dad, in fact. I very much miss him.

My parents did visit me in hospital and, when I finally left the hospital (I remember driving over Waterloo Bridge in the early evening, the aircon on, the radio in the taxi playing "In a Heartbeat" by Koop and thinking, yes, I might actually be happy again) I went down to Basingstoke to stay with them. I'd lost three stone in the hospital, and the first day I was down there they bought an Indian takeaway and a bottle of champagne. I was like a depleted forest being re-timbered. My mother couldn't wait to get the booze into me. I very much miss her too.

I got better, but the leg never properly healed. It was an inch shorter than it had been and still bent. The scar was a ten-inch sickle down my shin and to this day there's no sensation in the thin skin there. I lost a lot of lateral movement, so my tennis game suffered.

But I still have both legs. And I've never had to appear on *Strictly Come Dancing*. You have to roll with the positives.

I probably said it at the time, but thanks for looking after me, Chloe. I would probably have died without you. You nurtured me good.

A Baby Doc is always bad news . . .

THE SPINE WHO LOVED ME

      ⬧

𝕿HAT WAS quite a digression, but I think you're up to speed with my historical medical miseries. If you recall, twenty years after all the broken knee business, I'm living in a different country, I've been doing low impact exercise on an NHS yoga mat that smells of ass, and I'm about to have my last Pilates session.

There are four of us left. We few, we happy, brittle few. It's a fifty/fifty boy/girl split. Against all the odds the boys have achieved parity. I'm proud of Eddie and I. Caoilfhionn is back and handing out her stickers again. She knows who we are but it's a tradition now. It's our thing. We greedily accept them, noting her penmanship has trailed off a bit.

Today's session is a greatest hits package and we're all up for it. There is palpable camaraderie in the room. We made it, guys. Pilates whittled our squad down to a third, but when the cordite cleared, I was still standing among the ruins, which is how I refer to my fellow yoga practitioners. We work through hip twists, double leg stretches, shoulder bridges, scissors, clams, abductor lifts, and the cat. We barely creak. We are supple-adjacent. My arms feel strong, my shoulders seem to have widened. I'm barely sweating at all. My ruined limb hums with quiet agony, but when doesn't it? This is who I am now. I am a man who will spend the rest of his life lying on the spare room floor, breathing out, remaining zipped and hollowed, and slowly rebuilding his spine from the tail-bone up. Repeating up to five times.

Caoilfhionn makes an example of me. She brings me to the front of the class. She's trying to show how we're supposed to sink into our spines or something, and she illustrates this by pushing onto my chest and inviting me to *do the same to her.* Now, I've been coming here for six weeks, red-faced and sweaty and listening to my fellow practitioners groaning from both ends, and Caoilfhionn has stood at the front of the class, or while we're toiling clumsily on the floor, strolled around, correcting our postures, as though we were ornaments to the room. She seemed enormous, Olympian, an exemplar of youthful beauty in a room full of failing crocs. Standing in front of her and obliged to push her chest, I'm surprised by how small she is, how slight. She's like a ballet dancer, a gymnast. She probably was before she started doing this. I feel like Kong standing in front of Fay Wray, trying not to crush her. I place my hands just south of her collarbone and give a slight shove.

"What was that?" she says. "Give me a proper dig."

I give her a push. She's an immoveable object. She seems to be made of denser material than me. She's solidly rooted. I feel the energy of my push redirected down my arms. She shoves me in the tits. Hours later there will be two ghostly white hands clutching at the skin of my chest as I change t-shirts. It's like something you'd see if an exorcism wasn't going well.

At the end of the session Caoilfhionn wraps everything up. She talks about what we've learned and how this can enhance our lives going forward. I sit on the floor in front of her, gazing up. She's reliably Olympian again. I'm like a disciple at the foot of my master. Teach me, Guru. But she has nothing left to teach. It will be up to us now. We have used up our allotted chunk of NHS physical jerks.

I go outside into the grimness of Holywood Arches. But it isn't dark yet. Spring is coming. I stride home. Will I get the bus? Hell no. I walk back, effortlessly bipedal, back ramrod straight, head held high. Risky, with the state of the pavements in East Belfast.

BACK LAUNCH

———————————

I WAS AT another book launch. It was my own book launch. I'd written a book about my teeth and Sagging Meniscus Press had published it.

It's rare I don't complain. Things annoy me. That's what, in my experience, things do. They upset, they thwart, they hamper. They get all up in your grille. It's death by a thousand cuts, the slow accumulation of minor irritations, consolidating into an immovable boulder of rage I'm obliged to nudge up a hill, daily.

Half a century of this, fifty years of noticing and niggling. It's exhausting. Even good things come with a side order of irritation, an undertow of vexation, a soupçon of chagrin.

Except launching my book, *Teeth*, at The Black Box in Belfast. It was joyous. I was interviewed by my friend Shauna, and we were charming, funny, and insightful. I read well. The audience were delightful and there were a lot of them—standing room only. I sold all my books. I didn't even mind when they started using flashbulbs while I was trying to read my funny jokes out loud, slowly. That seems to be my style. Somewhere between Neil Gaiman and Stewart Lee: whispery, sibilant, ironic, disappointed. Droll scum.

After the ten-minute point, after I'd done my first reading, (at a lectern, because THEATRE, DARLING) I sat down and realised this was the most natural thing in the world. Sitting there chatting to a pal on a microphone in front of a paying audience who were laughing at my jokes . . . how is this the first time I've ever done this? Surely, I should've been doing this forever. It was fun. And crucially—after the previous week's testing visit to BAFTA, over which we'll draw a shroud (BUT MY GOD, WHAT A FARCE!)—it's a soothing balm to my ego. It was the rarest thing in my life—a thing I could do well. I'm someone quite often defeated by doorhandles and seatbelts, but here I was talking amusingly to a friendly crowd about a book I had written. It was brilliant. Finally, unalloyed joy.

Then I saw the photos.

Yeah.

I mean, really, *Teeth* is a book about my vanity. If I'm honest, although this book is about trying to fix my ruined spine, I had hoped there'd be a side order of me losing weight and looking great. It would be odd if I suddenly stopped being a self-regarding narcissist just because I'd bought a winning smile and learned how to rub my shoulders on the carpet.

But bloody hell. What happened to me? Why do I look like THAT?

I would say this: a) Shauna is a very slender, glamorous woman and I suffered by the comparison, and b) a pink spotlight? Really? On a sweaty, white guy? I've never looked so angry-of-*Question-Time* in my life.

There's not a single photo from the entire afternoon where I look anything less than hideous. I'm a Wall's sausage pressed into a corduroy shirt and stippled with white hair. And I'm lucky to have the hair.

Yes, I looked terrible and had no idea. But I refuse to let a thing like that spoil an otherwise joyous event. I'm back off the booze, and today, as Susan and I went for a walk, we discovered a gym. We went in. Outdoor swimming pool. Pilates.

Reader, I joined a fucking gym!

I mean to sculpt this sweaty brie, hone this melting-ice-cream physique. I don't want much, I just want to have a neck again. That's not greedy. Is it? A neck and a powerful core. A neck and freedom from spinal twinges. A neck and a belly that doesn't look as if I should be leaking milk from cracked nipples as I enter the third trimester. I want a back tapering at the waist into hard pockets of muscle like the puckered arms of a Chester-field, before fanning like a peacock's tail into shoulders so wide my epaulets are never in the same room at the same time.

I don't think that's too much to ask.

I spent a couple of weeks swimming, to build up my strength and stamina. The slow swimmer's lane is always empty because the sort of people who go to the gym are never going to be happy being seen as slow swimmers. These are highly motivated, competitive winners, which is why I've not spoken to a single human being since I joined the club. The initial financial outlay was enormous—two annual memberships—so I feel guilty if I don't go, like a wanton spendthrift, who might as well be thrusting the money into a stripper's G-string for all the good it's doing him. So, I've been going every other day.

And I felt pretty good. My clothes were starting to look a bit better on me, my posture was better. The aches and pains in my wrist and knee seemed to subside with the water's resistance. I'm a bad swimmer, and I don't like being peeled and blind in public, especially where there are hard surfaces and compromised friction. And the confident nudity of older men in the changing rooms is disturbing, all that parchment yellow, the rhubarb purples. The surprising patches of missing hair. But generally, I'm left alone in my lane to doggy-paddle from one end to the other, every length feeling like an achievement, every length representing something I haven't done before. It feels like progress. Slow, incremental, exhausting progress, and afterwards, after initial mild nausea, I feel fantastic. My body sings. My eyes are red, and my hair matted with chlorine, but my skin, my muscles are in glorious voice. Is this the body electric Walt Whitman was on about? Yeah. Sort of. Previously my body had been a runabout, something clapped-out and unobtrusive, a vehicle to get me from A to B without too much fuss. Yes, it was falling apart, rusted and corroded. I'd long suspected a dodgy solenoid or the possibility my big end was on the way out—I don't drive, this extended metaphor has been gleaned entirely from car insurance adverts—but it didn't really matter. There'd been a couple of big blow-outs but mostly it kept ticking over.

No more. I was pimping my ride. Spoiler alert.

I get three goes with a personal trainer as part of my membership and, after a fortnight of swimming, felt I'd built up the stamina to do an assisted gym session. In truth, the availability of these freebies runs out after the first month, and I would have been quite happy to let it. But I'd been to a wedding, and someone had filmed me dancing without my knowledge. In the moment, I was thinking, "You've still got it, John. Sweet feet. My arse is a blur—it's like a bee's wing. They'll be naming this dance-floor after me."

What I saw on the video resembled a portly, middle-aged vicar in the throes of a psychotropic freak-out, his black barrel body shooting out limbs as though trapped in some personal hokey-cokey hell. Clearly, I would have to step up the gym regime.

This is the second time unposed-for video footage has caused me to make changes in my lifestyle. It really is an incredible resource. A withering, dispiriting resource.

I met up with my trainer in the gym. She's slightly older than me but we're very different shapes. She glows with ectomorph positivity, a beaming, flesh-coloured skeleton in hi-vis Lycra. We shake hands and I tell her I'm nervous, which I'm not, but I often blurt out random things in awkward social situations. I wish I hadn't. It becomes the baseline for our relationship. She thinks I'm terrified of gyms and spends the next hour saying "Don't be nervous. I can see you're nervous. There's no need—I'm here."

She doesn't ask me about my health goals so, midway through my first go on a low impact treadmill called the *Woodway*, I offer the following:

"Yeah, I'm really all about strengthening my core, doing some low-resistance stuff for my knees, lower back, that sort of thing . . ."

She looks me up and down, and says, "Yeah, we'll do some cardio so you can lose weight," adding, unconvincingly, "for your posture."

I make jokes throughout the session which she takes as an admission of weakness, probably a shrewd assessment of comedy's raison d'etre, but you don't want it from a personal trainer. She didn't seem to have a sense of humour at all, something you often find with people who espouse a philosophy of positivity. They tend to blink with one eye like a lizard, and grin till their teeth dry when you crack a joke. They're aware something's been said but are unable to process it. Comedy comes from negativity, from weakness and fallibility. From pain. Lift a rock, and you'll see all the comedy wriggling about beneath it, in the dark stuff.

At one point she has me sit on a rubber ball with two skipping rope handles in my hands pretending to ski. The gym is another country; they do things stupidly there.

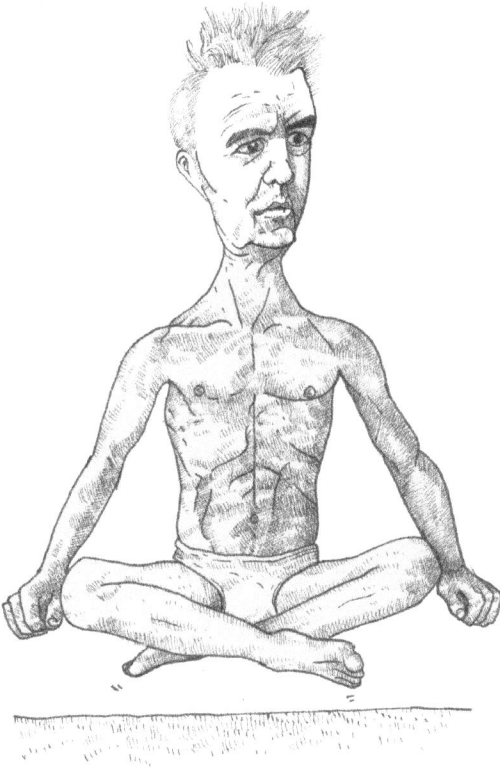

You too can have a body like mine (if you employ an illustrator with no knowledge of human anatomy)

We finished on the ropes (literally). I'd seen this on the telly—people squatting and snaking two twelve-foot ropes across the floor—but I never thought I'd live to do it. I've played with battle ropes, I've met David Soul, I've won a prize for growing a massive sunflower, and I've had sex with a Canadian. No one can tell me I've not lived.

It was fine. I've booked another session of middle-aged panic for next week. My back, my knee, my poor arthritic wrist are in good hands. I feel fitter and stronger than I have in years, and my trainer has promised me at some point I will lose some weight, my knee will straighten, my posture will improve, and my back will be loadbearing and certain, a fulsome fulcrum.

And if I lose my sense of humour, it's all to the good. Like being unshackled from a lunatic.

Good riddance, chuckles.

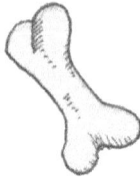

GL-OSSUARY

4 **fermented fish guts** — Garum was made by fermenting ungutted fish in the hot sun with salt. Cooks added honey, herbs and wine to make it palatable. They failed. You can see why Rome declined now: taverna waiter, "Fermented fish guts, sir?" Roman citizen, "I decline."

6 **medical leeches** — I've had experience of medical leeches—raised under laboratory conditions and dyed blue so they stand out against the hot red of your insides—and they did a sterling job. Thanks for ridding me of infection, you greedy little surgeons. Hopefully they're humanely murdered afterwards—nobody needs a medical fly. Colonoscopy experts, no doubt.

6 **micturating freely over my French Fries** — this is a polite Americanisation of the British idiom *pissing on my chips*. Both are similar in meaning to the more common *raining on my parade*, though that expression is effectively meaningless in Northern Ireland where I live as, while there are many, many, parades, it is *always* raining.

7 **Paris number** — Yeah, the best I can do here is the following: "A client centred health record used in acute, community and long-term care homes." No idea what that has to do with Paris, though if you ring them the hold music is Juliet Greco live from the Olympia.

9 **The Bronze** — In *Buffy the Vampire Slayer*, the Bronze is an alcohol-free nightclub serving complicated coffees to the elderly students of Sunnydale High. It's a day-care centre with barely audible whine-core playing in the background. I would like to go on record as a big fan of *Buffy the Vampire Slayer*—I like jokes and folklore served up with roundhouse kicks to the face—it was sharp and funny and subversive, and therefore it was massively disappointing to hear about Joss Whedon's behaviour behind the scenes. Go Cordelia.

12 **the manosphere** — The manosphere is a cabal of bullshitting grifters radicalising virgins into thinking women are not people but assets to be acquired or destroyed. They value supercars, cigars, cage-fighting, Veet, sex trafficking and the oxygen of publicity. And Paypal, presumably. They are worthless scum and should be in prison. There will be jokes soon, I promise.

13 **Bat-mite and Ace, the Bat Hound** — Bat-mite was a fifth dimensional superfan of Batman, who would often contrive perilous scenarios just to watch his hero in action. He was retired in 1964 for being a bit shit. Ace, The Bat Hound was Batman's dog. Wikipedia lists his abilities as "agility" and "a keen sense of smell", which suggests Wikipedia is taking the piss. Ace, The Bat Hound wears a mask because, you know, he has a secret identity. Ace, The Bat Hound was retired in 1964 for being a bit shit.

13 *Theatre of Blood* — is the greatest film of all time. If you haven't seen it, you should see it. If you have seen it, you should put down this book and go and watch it again. I mean, you've reached the glossary. You're basically done here. Go, go and watch *Theatre of Blood*.

13 **Equity minimum** — Equity is the performing arts and entertainment trade union. Back when I was young and naïve—mid-forties—I established an amateur dramatics theatre company, mainly to expose the world to my GENIUS and, being principled, we elected to pay our actors Equity minimum, even though most of them weren't in Equity. We never did it again though, as it bankrupted us, and the company folded. I had to borrow money, and I was still paying it off a year later. Note to self: if you want to be ethical get some financial backing. Actor's agents are like ravening wolves.

17 **Evel Knievel** — a motorcycle stunt performer famous for leaping over rows of buses and then requiring extensive hospital treatment. More scar than man, Evel was chiefly famous in the Britain of my youth as an action figure. The hand-cranked Stunt Cycle—described as "gyro-power"—was the most exciting thing an English child had ever seen in 1973. When I inherited my cousin's Stunt Cycle, about six years after it was fashionable, it was STILL the most exciting thing I'd ever seen.

18 *Billy Elliot* — I haven't seen *Billy Elliot*, but as far as I can work out it's about a little boy who likes ballet but his widowed, miner father doesn't allow him to attend lessons. It's a bit like that scene in *Zoolander*, where gruff, suds-chugging Jon Voight watches his son, Derek, in a perfume advert. "I'm a Merman. A MERMAN!" I have seen *Zoolander*. I may even have seen the sequel but have retained not a single memory of it. Or was that *Anchorman*? "Chicken of the cave"? Is that it?

19 **Cain and Abel** — were like an olden days Gallagher brothers, and like the Gallagher brothers there's another brother, Seth, nobody's bothered about. In the story of Cain and Abel we discover that God is not vegetarian. This is the Old Testament God, of course. Jesus was famously pescatarian.

Cain was a grower of wheat, Abel a farmer of livestock. If both brothers had come together and invented the hamburger, this whole sorry mess could have been avoided. God loves a triple-stack.

20   **Orange Men** — The Loyal Orange Institution is a Protestant fraternal order based in Northern Ireland, founded in County Armagh in 1795. Some of the original founders appear to still be very active in the group and remain the enlightened architects of their policy. Orange Men wear bowler hats, sashes, carry furled umbrellas, and every July 12th march about Northern Ireland playing "The Auld Orange Flute" on drums and whistles, before relaxing in a field with a big bag of cans until they get sleepy.

23   **The Sun King** — Louis XIV was known as the Sun King for the opulence and splendour of his court. He was France's longest reigning monarch, and that record is unlikely to be broken any time soon. A hundred years after his death the eccentric English scientist William Buckland ate his partially mummified heart, apparently "for a laugh". *Sun King* is also the name of a minor *Beatles* song which starts sounding exactly like Fleetwood Mac's *Albatross*, before turning into every 10cc song ever. Except *Dreadlock Holiday*. That one sounds like the middle eight in *Live and Let Die*.

25   **Can's *Future Days*** — Can were a band from Cologne in Germany. They're exalted in Kosmische Musik circles and *Future Days* may be my favourite of their records. It's tumultuous, oceanic music, with Damo Suzuki's keening, sensual voice like a raft borne high on the swollen water. Would heartily recommend. Also, *Moonshake* has a sequence that sounds like someone hitting cuddly toys with a toffee hammer.

29   **"Bartleby the Scrivener"** — is a short story by Herman Melville about a lawyer hiring a clerk who, though initially able to do a great deal of high-quality work, eventually declines to do anything at all and, when asked, simply says "I would prefer not to". Eventually, his preferring not to extends to eating and he starves to death. "Bartleby, the Scrivener" is, approximately, the story of the first forty years of my life.

30   **The Oak Island Mystery** — Oak Island is off the coast of Nova Scotia. The original mystery concerned the piratical Captain Kydd and his ill-gotten gains, but latterly the treasure has evolved into anything you want it to be: the Ark of the Covenant, a lost Shakespearian manuscript, the entrance to a subterranean paradise, the final resting place of Jimmy Hoffa, the missing Wicker Man film cans, the shoe my brother threw in the sea when I was ten and I had to walk home with only

one shoe and it was me that got into trouble because *it can't always be the baby* but it could, because it always *was* the baby, every single time it was the baby, or the Holy Grail.

Hell of a throwing arm on that baby.

35 *An American Werewolf in London* — Americans disregard English country bylaws and come to a sticky end. A sticky, hairy, bitey end.

37 **retrieving a rubber brick from the bottom of the pool while wearing your pyjamas** — in the 1970s and '80s this is how British schoolchildren earned swimming certificates. I don't know why. It may still happen, I don't know. What do you expect me to do? Research? You sicken me.

37 **Tiamat** — is the Mesopotamian Goddess representing the Primordial Sea. That's quite hard to find out on the internet though, because she's also apparently a *Dungeons and Dragons* character, and you have to wade through thickets of guff to get anywhere near the original *she who bore them all*. I have no beef with D and D players. I'm a nerd. I'm just not a twelve-sided dice kind of nerd.

38 **Bodyform** — is a feminine intimate care product, advertised in the early '90s by women leaping from planes, driving convertibles through deserts, or chasing after packs of dogs on roller-skates, while a gravel-voiced rock chanteuse extolled the virtues of menstruation. I was almost jealous of the fabulous time women seemed to be having on their period, but when I said this out loud to my female friends, they hit me in the head with rocks. Quite right.

41 **grasp the nettle** — means taking confident, decisive action, based on the premise that if you firmly take hold of a nettle it will not sting you, as though the nettle is quietly impressed by your leadership skills and business mettle. No, the nettle will just sting you. You don't get the benefit of the doubt from a nettle. It has a job to do, and that job is to raise welts on your naked palm. A nettle's not fucking about.

42 **Nurples so purple** — a purple nurple is one of the least sophisticated moves in the bully's repertoire, being just an aggressive twist of the mamilla between thumb and forefinger, as though relieving a bolt of its nut. Eventually, bruising or bleeding might occur, and your lunch money is secured. If you don't know what I'm talking about, we had very different childhoods.

46 *The Red Shoe Diaries* — a TV show featuring Fox Mulder and his dog, Stella, placing an advert in a newspaper asking women to confess their sexual awakenings to him in letters he reads by railway cuttings or sat by a brazier in a junkyard, for

some reason. Women do reply, and '90s smut doyen, Zalman King, films it, with a lot of blue gel and the saxophone solo from *Careless Whisper*. There are lots of shots of the shadows of electric fans and diaphanous curtains and Audie England's bee-stung lips. Unadulterated '90s cowards' porn.

51 **the A.A.** — this is the Automobile Association, as opposed to Alcoholics Anonymous. Just so we're clear. The vehicular A.A. is based in my hometown of Basingstoke, and working in the Fanum House offices was a regular rite of passage for the town's cannon-fodder youth, rather like that bit in *A Man Called Horse* where Richard Harris is hung from the roof of a teepee by his nipples. *Fanum* is the Latin for *Temple* and was chosen to show the A.A. is the nation's leading breakdown service, which it spectacularly fails to do.

55 **Glider Halt** — in Belfast this is the name of the place where the buses—Gliders—stop. Or halt. The glider-halts have an interesting feature. There are two rows of seats, one with three raised metal arms between the seats, and one set at an angle, so you can lean against it, instead of sitting. This innovation in seating technology is so homeless people can't sleep on the benches. Lovely. And what do they want sleep for anyway? They'd just spend it on drugs.

60 *Fame* — Sigh. *Fame*. Leaping over yellow cabs and fire hydrants in leg warmers or pirouetting in front of someone holding a ghetto blaster over their head, the mounted police powerless in the face of all this exuberant talent. You know? You know.

65 **"Space Age Bachelor Pad Music"** — from the *Stereolab* mini-album *The Groop Played Space Age Bachelor Pad Music*. But we would have been listening to a variety of things under that umbrella: *Esquivel* and *Les Baxter*, *Betty Boo* and *Dee-lite*, *The High Llamas* and *Saint Etienne*, *Stan Getz* and *Astrud Gilberto* and *Dmitri from Paris*. The cocktails never ran out until someone was hospitalised. On this occasion it was me. It was usually me.

69 *On the Town with The League of Gentlemen* — *The League of Gentlemen* were a comic troupe of actor/writers, whose fictional Northern English town, Royston Vasey, proved a wellspring of comic invention. They are modern Gillrays, purveyors of Grand Guignol grotesquerie and comedic chops to the windpipe. This was their first radio show, before they made the move to television, and they're slightly un-cooked here—Royston Vasey is still called Spent, and there's a character who's just a tiny tobacconist, and that's it—but it's brilliantly funny and beautifully observed and made sure the tears on my hospital pillow were tears of laughter, occasionally.

71 **the Hippocratic oath** — *Primum non nocere*, "first do no harm". Obviously, the American version is *Primum reprehendo cautionum*, "first check the insurance". (Apologies to any native speakers for the poor quality of my Latin).

74 **canoeing at Symond's Yat** — Symonds Yat is a village in Herefordshire, and one of best places in England to see peregrine falcons. It's also one of the best places in the country to watch red-faced, captains of industry drown, as they're a) hypercompetitive and b) not going to listen to some college pudding tell them how to drive a fucking canoe.

75 **Mad Frankie Fraser** — Frankie Fraser called himself a "rascal", but what he really was was a violent gangster thug with a propensity for removing people's teeth with pliers. In his later years, he re-invented himself as a media celebrity, which fitted with the *Lock, Stock and Two Smoking Barrels* laddism of the late '90s and led to a cultural ethos where the loudest bloke in the pub is a "character" and the biggest bully a "legend". It's why we now elect Prime Ministers because "they seem like a laugh". None of this is Frankie's fault. As mentioned, he's now safely dead and, if I believed in hell, he'd be there having infinite toothy pegs ripped from his ribboned gums by a *rascal* with hooves and a pointy tail.

78 **a Swanee whistle** — is a slide whistle, the pitch of the instrument being changed by moving the slide plunger in and out, producing ascending and descending glisses. In English films of the 1970s this is the noise that implies a foreign object has been inserted into the rectum. It's usually accompanied by a close-up of the recipient's face, expressing concern.

78 **Kenneth Williams** — that face would often be Kenneth Williams'. Actor, diarist, raconteur, and suicide, Kenny lived a tortured life, one of a generation of misfit actors that drifted into the *Carry on* films because they had nowhere else to go. Kenny hated the franchise but kept taking the cheque, which was £5000 in 1958 for *Carry on Sergeant* and was still £5000 twenty-one years later for *Carry on Emmanuelle*.

82 **oomska** — meaning filth, dirt, and perhaps from a pig Latin form of *scum*. It was popularised by the endlessly quotable film, *Withnail and I*, and uttered by Uncle Monty, (Richard Griffiths) perhaps the most loved theatrical, predatory homosexual in British cinematic history, mostly because he is fictional. The British love a big, fruity queer, so long as he's safely contained by the television or cinema screen. It's the free-range ones they have a problem with.

86 *Horace Goes Skiing* — Horace was a small blue man who had to navigate a busy road in order the rent some skis. He then went skiing. This was a video game for

people who owned ZX Spectrum computers, who were people who had no interest in computers except for playing games. I failed to nurture any coding skills, but I made damn sure Horace got his money's worth out of those rented skis.

90 **Douglas Bader** — Air Force flying ace from World War II, who lost both his legs doing aerobatics (showing off). He learned to fly again with painful prosthetic legs and had a successful war. Portrayed as a bellowing oaf by Kenneth More (More's standard characterisation) in the film *Reach for the Sky*, the real Bader seems to have been a bellowing oaf too, though more inclined to swearing. He liked apartheid, capital punishment, and wrote the foreword to the book *Stuka Pilot* by Hans Ulrich Rudel, a fervent Nazi supporter. Never-the-less, he could fly a plane with no legs, so well done him.

90 *Strictly Come Dancing* — a British reality TV show where female celebrities are abused, verbally and physically, until they learn to dance.

91 **The Magic Circle** — is a club for lonely people with a lot of free time and a lot of patience. Nowadays, they'd just be on-line, trolling Taylor Swift; the find-the-lady *de nos jours*.

99 **Neil Gaiman** — I resemble Neil Gaiman in the slow, whispery, sibilance of my voice. And in no other way AT ALL.

100 *Question Time* — a venerable BBC topical discussion show, in which four right-wing populists attempt to rile up the jowl-quivering red-faced men in the audience, even though they're already furious, mainly about immigration. You could shoot a dirigible into space with the sheer amount of hot air produced.

106 **David Soul** — actor, singer, and a man I had a piss next to in a North London pub in 2005. He played Hutch in *Starsky and Hutch* and the writer turned vampire slayer in *Salem's Lot*, an obvious career progression. He seemed pretty cool. Excellent urinal etiquette.

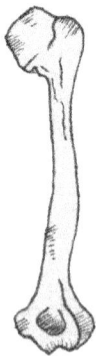

ACKNOWLEDGEMENTS

This book received baffled but helpful notes from Tyler C. Gore and Jacob Smullyan, and the always careful attentions of Guillermo Stitch. Parts of the ending have been stitched together from Chloe Travers' rather splintered recollections—reassuringly on message, there—and she remains the reason I can still stand on my own two feet.

Thanks to Susan Garnett, who makes all things possible all the time.

John Patrick Higgins is a writer and director. He is the author of *Teeth* and *Fine* (both 2024, Sagging Meniscus). He lives in Belfast, where it rains.

www.ingramcontent.com/pod-product-compliance
Ingram Content Group UK Ltd.
Pitfield, Milton Keynes, MK11 3LW, UK
UKHW031045110425
457305UK00003B/4

9 781963 846348